Ace the Corporate Personality Test

Ace the Corporate Personality Test

Edward Hoffman

McGraw-Hill

New York   San Francisco   Washington, D.C.   Auckland   Bogotá
Caracas   Lisbon   London   Madrid   Mexico City   Milan
Montreal   New Delhi   San Juan   Singapore
Sydney   Tokyo   Toronto

Library of Congress Cataloging-in-Publication Data

Hoffman, Edward.
    Ace the corporate personality test / Edward Hoffman.
      p. cm.
    Includes bibliographical references.
    ISBN 0-07-135912-5
    1. Personality and occupation.   2. Prediction of occupational success.
    3. Employees—Psychological testing.   4. Work—Psychological aspects.
    5. Personality tests.   I. Title.

BF698.9.03 H63 2000
650.14—dc21   00-061659

McGraw-Hill

A Division of The McGraw·Hill Companies

1 2 3 4 5 6 7 8 9 0 DOC/DOC 0 9 8 7 6 5 4 3 2 1 0

ISBN 0-07-135912-5

This book was set in Palatino by North Market Street Graphics. Printed and bound by R.R. Donnelley & Sons Company.

This publication is designed to provide accurate and authoritative information in regard to the subject matter covered. It is sold with the understanding that neither the author nor the publisher is engaged in rendering legal, accounting, or other professional service. If legal advice or other expert assistance is required, the services of a competent professional person should be sought.
      —From a Declaration of Principles jointly adopted by a Committee of the American Bar Association and a Committee of Publishers.

McGraw-Hill books are available at special quantity discounts to use as premiums and sales promotions, or for use in corporate training programs. For more information, please write to the Director of Special Sales, McGraw-Hill, Professional Publishing, Two Penn Plaza, New York, NY 10121-2298. Or contact your local bookstore.

 This book is printed on recycled, acid-free paper containing a minimum of 50% recycled de-inked fiber.

To the memory of my teacher Edwin Karpf

Contents

Mental Health Disclaimer   ix

Acknowledgments   xi

Part I   An Overview of Personality Measurement

1   Today's Testing Boom   3

2   What Is Personality?   7

3   Personality Testing: Then and Now   13

4   Mental Probing by Interview   19

5   Mastering the Test-Taking Procedure   27

6   The Lie Scale: Fielding "Softball" Questions   31

Part II   Specific Realms of Assessment

7   Conscientiousness: Can You Be Absolutely Counted On?   37

8   Extraversion: Are You the Life of the Party?   45

9   Integrity: Are You Honest as the Day Is Long?   53

10   Going Postal: Are You Feeling Angry?   61

11   Are You Entrepreneurial?   69

12   Stress Tolerance: Can You Keep Your Cool?   77

13   Leadership: Do You Have the Right Stuff?   **85**

14   Beating Test Jitters   **93**

Part III   Six Sample Personality Tests

Test-Taking Instructions   **99**

    Sample Personality Test 1, 100
    Sample Personality Test 2, 107
    Sample Personality Test 3, 115
    Sample Personality Test 4, 123
    Sample Personality Test 5, 131
    Sample Personality Test 6, 139

Glossary   **149**

References   **153**

Index   **155**

Mental Health Disclaimer

The purpose of this book is solely to acquaint readers with personality assessment in the hiring process today. The practice test items and scoring interpretations I have provided are not intended in any way to provide actual diagnostic or clinical help, guidance, or direction for anyone who may read this book. Persons who are experiencing emotional difficulties, whether job-related or otherwise, are advised to see a licensed mental health professional immediately for accurate diagnosis and intervention.

Acknowledgments

Though this book had been germinating in conceptual form for several years, it was editor Griffin Hansbury of McGraw-Hill who provided the encouragement for its growth to fruition. The editorial judgment of Susan Barry at McGraw-Hill was also instrumental in bringing this project to the attention of my literary agent, Alice Martell. I am appreciative of her expert guidance from start to finish.

Over the years, I've enjoyed many stimulating conversations with Fanny Cheng, Professor Eric Freedman, Aaron Hostyk, Dr. Ted Mann, Dr. Samuel Menahem, Paul Palnik, Dr. Russ Reeves, K. Dean Stanton, and Alyce Tresenfeld on educational and psychological topics central to this book. These dialogues have been a major source of inspiration to me. As research assistants, Harvey Gitlin and Linda Joyce have been eager and efficient.

I am also grateful for my family's interest and enthusiasm during this entire project.

PART 1

An Overview of Personality Measurement

1
Today's Testing Boom

Well, you've finally earned your degree and are now seeking your first professional position. Or, perhaps you've held such employment for several years and are ready to embark on a serious job-hunt for advancement. Or, maybe you're switching fields, or else returning to the working world after a significant break. In any of these instances, it's likely that you'll be taking a personality test before getting hired. And you know what?

Despite the importance—even the *make-or-break* nature of the interview and testing procedure—you probably haven't a clue as to what it's all about.

This observation isn't meant to be critical, so don't take it personally or berate yourself. Unless you've majored in psychology and taken at least a course or two in testing, it's unlikely that you would be knowledgeable on this subject—specific information about workplace personality assessment is notoriously difficult for ordinary persons to obtain. Yes, the details exist and can be found, but knowing how to use these constructively for your own benefit would take an advanced psychology degree—as well as a specialty in current methodology. But relax: I have precisely such training—coupled with twenty years of testing experience—and have evaluated thousands of children and adults. My goal, therefore, is to provide you with a simple, down-to-earth, and relevant guide to personality testing in today's business world—particularly as it relates to the hiring process.

For many reasons, it's increasingly likely that candidates will be required to take a personality test before being hired. Often, they will also be expected to take related instruments periodically on the job, for management or leadership training, for example, or for promotion into high-tech/start-up divisions within well-established large companies. While personality tests have been used by employers for over eighty years, the field is expanding as never before. Why is this so?

Dramatic improvement in the tests themselves is a primary factor. Mathematical breakthroughs coupled with advanced computer technology have made these tests a lot more powerful statistically than in the past. As a result, they can far more accurately differentiate highly desirable job applicants, highly unappealing ones, and all those in between.

Second, the tests are much improved conceptually. Dating back to the influence of psychiatrist Sigmund Freud nearly a century ago, many personality instruments were based on theories about human development that are now as outdated as typewriters and vinyl records. Among the most notorious was the "Blacky Test" from the 1950s, which, based on psychoanalytic notions of infant sexuality and the Oedipus Complex, required people to respond to drawings presenting Blacky the Dog in arguments, conflicts, and sexual longings relating to his family members. Presumably, the stories individuals gave in response to these unwittingly bizarre pictures would reveal important aspects about their own personality.

Not surprisingly, such tests had meager value for employers concerned with practical matters of employee absenteeism, theft, productivity, teamwork, and leadership. As late as the mid-1970s some researchers doubted whether psychology would ever be of real help to organizations seeking reliable instruments in hiring and promoting workers. But all that has changed dramatically in recent years; as you'll see in Chapters Two and Three, sophistication in the field has been steadily increasing.

A third factor in the current significance of testing is the growth of computers, which has made test scoring, and even administering, much more user-friendly. Increasingly, within seconds after a candidate completes his or her personality questionnaire via a computer hookup to the Internet, the answers are tabulated and scored—and a detailed profile is printed out for the interviewer. Based exclusively on the candidate's answers, the profile is even accompanied with specific recommendations to: *Hire, Do Not Hire,* or *Maybe Hire.* On this basis, the interviewer can welcome the candidate into the personnel office for a detailed interview and related job discussion—or, instead politely offer the kiss-off and verbal kiss-of-death: "Thank you for coming today. We'll be in touch."

Fourthly, in our fast-paced and technological society today, companies are increasingly forced to rely on psychological tests in the absence of other data. For example, it's now typical for most employers to refrain from providing detailed reference letters on current or past employees—due to fear of being sued should they prove incompetent or dishonest at the new position. Companies also fear that a disgruntled employee might sue for defamation of character. In most situations now, therefore, organizations will merely state: "Jennifer Olsen worked as marketing assistant for three years" and refrain from offering any specific remarks about her character, talents, and weaknesses. For precisely this reason, information gleaned from personality tests today can be important, even crucial, in the hiring process.

Finally, personality tests have proven helpful in the crucial domains of management and leadership training. As organizations become increasingly interested in retaining and promoting employees from within, such training has become a significant enterprise. To make it as empirically rigorous as possible, the use of personality tests has greatly expanded. For instance, the Myers-

Briggs Personality Inventory—based on the "type" theory of psychiatrist Carl Jung—has proven especially popular in recent years, alone generating annual sales of over $3.5 million for its publisher.

Indeed, the sheer financial size of the testing industry nowadays shows the seriousness with which employers are taking personality tests. In a word, they are cost effective: particularly for screening out highly undesirable potential workers. While most executives and upper-level managers realize that these tests are far from infallible, they're increasingly mandatory in hiring for many types of positions, and are prized for other situations, like management or leadership training.

There's absolutely no indication, therefore, that this trend will end. Indeed, the growth of computer technology and Internet access makes it ever more likely that personality testing will only gain in importance.

Given this probability, can you actually benefit from "coaching" on such tests? Just as with the College Board and Educational Testing Service companies that market the SATs, personality test developers want you to believe that coaching is useless—or at best, of minimal assistance. But the cold truth is that practice *does* help. Psychological research has shown that people can effectively alter their performance on personality tests, and that it's not even very difficult.

Is it ethical to "prepare" or "get coached" for personality tests in the business world? Well, it's certainly not illegal. But let's look at it this way: If you're a shy person who prefers solitary activities, is it sensible to misrepresent yourself as the "life of the party"? Clearly, if you're applying for a sales job involving a lot of "cold calls," and you're basically introverted, it's a waste of everyone's time—including yours—to portray yourself as outgoing and gregarious. You may get hired, but how successful will you actually be on the job?

But it certainly can't hurt to know the tester's goals, reasoning, and expectations when you sit down to take a personality test at your next job candidacy. The choice, of course, is yours. In my opinion, it's important for a level playing field to exist between recruiter and applicant—especially in the absence of privacy and confidentiality safeguards.

Moreover, the caveat in the business world today is that company loyalty and guarantees for longtime employment are totally gone. Rather, you're now the manager of your own career, and as such, personality testing ought to be a definite part of your knowledge base.

What legal safeguards do you have in this domain? Unfortunately, the answer is almost none. At all levels, courts have been extremely reluctant about getting involved in the hiring and supervising details of organizational life. There's basically just one major rule: *A psychological test must not discriminate on the basis of race, religion, national origin, gender, or sexual orientation.*

In this regard, the courts have further decreed that the burden of proof lies with the employer or test user; that is, before administering a test of honesty, the employer must know that it does not unfairly discriminate against, say, racial minorities or women. For example, test items that probe a person's belief in

Jesus Christ, Moses, or Mohammed, would almost certainly be viewed as discriminatory. So, most likely, would those that measure attitudes toward varieties of sexual behavior.

But generally, courts have allowed employers a very wide latitude in terms of questions—as long as they're not discriminatory and have some conceivable bearing on employee productivity. Thus, there are many personality items that assess your attitudes, values, and goals in life—and what really matters to you.

What happens to your results once you've taken the test? The bad news is that you have much less legal protection than you think. Especially with the advent of computer databases, the answers that you provide about your innermost self can be converted into a computer file (often the tests are directly administered on-line anyway) and then stored indefinitely, as well as made available to other potential employers.

Many job applicants don't seem to mind this situation, or at least try not to think about it. They regard most test questions as rather benign, not particularly intrusive, and that may be fine. But be aware that what you respond will not necessarily be tossed into the garbage after your interview; it may well become part of a national database available to private employers, and conceivably also to advertisers, researchers, and anyone willing to pay the fee. What if you refuse to take a personality test? Of course, you always have that option, and you may conceivably be able to negotiate that with a potential employer. But you also may be rejected from all further consideration for the position.

In our new century, becoming "test-wise" psychologically may be one of your most important career assets. The times are changing in many ways, from globalization to the nature of work itself. As the recent adage affirms: "Information is power, information is money"—just as time is money. The more information you have—especially about the basics of personality testing in the workplace—the greater control you have over your own career.

By the end of this book, you'll not only have learned some things about yourself that might be useful in career and specific job planning, but also have acquired a thorough understanding of what employers are really seeking with these instruments. These are my goals in writing this volume, and I hope that together we'll be successful.

2
What Is Personality?

People exhibit very different qualities in everyday life. Some of us like loud parties, and others prefer quiet get-togethers. Some of us have lots of friends, and others are basically loners. Some crave constant change and novelty, and others desire stability and routine. Some of us become easily stressed, and others are hard to rattle. Some persons push themselves relentlessly in daily life, and others are laid back. Some strive for wealth or fame, and others embrace modest goals. Some of us are entranced by music, art, or literature, and others find these boring.

What accounts for such fascinating variability among people? That's a key focus of the science of *personality*: that unique and enduring bundle of traits, attitudes, motivations, behavioral tendencies, and needs that makes each of us who we are. But how do these qualities originate? Do they result from our childhood upbringing, or they are inborn in nature? How stable are they? Are they permanent, or can they alter dramatically—such as at certain specific stages of life? At what age do children start showing distinct traits? Do men and women actually have different personalities when it comes to love and intimacy, or is all this talk about "Mars and Venus" just a lot of interplanetary hot air?

Such questions have intrigued social scientists for more than a hundred years. The key figures in defining what we call "personality" were Europeans Sigmund Freud, Carl Jung, and Alfred Adler, and they achieved world fame and influence during the early decades of the twentieth century for their theories and therapeutic methods. Though differing from one another in their specific notions, all three broadly argued that personality is formed by the age of six, greatly resists change thereafter, and is almost entirely the result of parenting, especially maternal. This outlook became known as *psychodynamic*, referring to dynamic or changeable aspects within us emotionally.

During this same period, a second influential "school" of personality emerged, known as *behaviorist*. Led by the American psychologist John Watson, and later by B. F. Skinner, behaviorism insisted that our personality is a "blank slate" at birth and that everything that makes us individually distinct is due to the mix of stimuli and resulting reinforcement (that is, reward or punishment) for our responses.

A third "school" of human personality was founded by motivational theorist Abraham Maslow. As early as the mid-1940s he argued that both the psychodynamic and behaviorist views were partly correct, but that more importantly, all human beings share a biologically based "core" of needs, values, goals, satisfactions, and frustrations. Emphasized today in managerial and marketing courses, as well as psychology, Maslow's system affirms that these inborn tendencies exist in a hierarchy encompassing safety, belongingness, esteem and respect, love, and self-actualization.

Maslow's powerful approach, known as *humanistic* because it stresses individual uniqueness, has recently been buttressed by the growth of biological psychology coupled with genetics. As a result, a strong consensus about human personality has recently emerged. Let's briefly focus on three aspects that will help you to better understand what this vital concept is all about.

1. HOW EARLY DOES OUR PERSONALITY FORM?

The originators of modern personality study clearly saw that young children are quite different in their behavioral styles. While some are shy and timid, others are outgoing and even assertive. Some youngsters greatly enjoy schoolwork and are academically ambitious, whereas others prefer drawing, music, or athletics. Founding figures like Freud, Jung, and Adler also recognized that some children exhibited serious emotional problems, like constant anger, aggression, or fearfulness. While such observations were useful at the time, these were generally anecdotal and lacked objectivity and "hard data" involving large numbers of youngsters.

Today, the study of *temperament*—the biological foundation of personality— has significantly impacted upon personality theory and research. Based on extensive "child laboratory" observation and probing interviews with parents, psychologists now know that newborn infants vary greatly with regard to such important traits as emotional reactivity, intensity and quality of mood, the amount of exploratory behavior they exhibit, ease of "warming up," adaptability, and sociability.

These qualities have been linked to personality differences in later childhood, adolescence, and adulthood. For example, babies who are timid about exploring their cribs seem to become adults who are more anxious and apprehensive about taking risks. Similarly, infants who react fearfully to strangers appear likely to be shy and introverted as grown-ups.

Such research clearly shows that human personality is not a "blank slate" at birth, as behaviorists like Watson and Skinner stressed; and, contrary as well to the psychodynamic viewpoint, we all show major personality differences before the parenting process has even begun to influence us. Indeed, psychologists now believe that parents act differently according to their youngsters' own temperaments, and that our adult personality is probably half due to our individual biological makeup and half to our day-to-day experiences involving parents, siblings, friends, relatives and neighbors, school, television, movies, and other aspects of our social milieu.

Interestingly, some theorists believe that our most important early environment is our mother's womb, where most of us spend approximately nine months exposed to a constant flow of hormones through her bloodstream via the placenta. Such psychologists argue that if the mother is constantly angry, stressed, or fearful, the specific hormones these emotions release into the fetus's bloodstream may exert a lifetime impact.

How about genetic influence on temperament and personality? The consensus today is that the fifty percent of our personality to which biology contributes results from many small additive aspects, and that, despite what you may read in the Sunday newspaper or hear on television, there is probably no "single gene" for traits like diligence, ambition, friendliness, creativity, empathy, moodiness, or sexuality.

The field of temperament is still quite young, but it's now possible to say that personality differences are apparent as early as birth, and that by middle childhood—the elementary school years—the basis of our personality is strongly, though not completely, evidenced and formed. For example, work-related traits like conscientiousness and achievement motivation are apparent by kindergarten and the lower elementary school grades, as are the qualities of gregariousness, proneness to anger, and low tolerance for stress. There's even evidence that entrepreneurialism and leadership during adulthood can be predicted by youngsters' behaviors in early to middle childhood.

2. DOES OUR PERSONALITY CHANGE?

The entire fields of psychotherapy and counseling are based on the perspective that as adults we can certainly change our attitudes, behavioral tendencies, and goals in life. Many different approaches to personality change exist, but they all insist that movement and growth are possible during adulthood. However, psychologists also believe that it becomes harder for us to change our personality as we get older; and, when change does occur, it's almost always a modification, rather than a huge alteration, of our inner "core."

Today, counseling and therapy are mainly designed, therefore, to help the individual function better in terms of *who he or she is,* rather than trying to effect a total "makeover." So if you're feeling lonely and are basically a shy person, you won't be expected to dominate boisterous parties as a result of therapeutic help. Rather, the emphasis will be on helping you to create friendship and intimacy through quiet, one-on-one or small-group activities consistent with who you are.

Interestingly, within the field of *psychometrics* (psychological testing) this viewpoint has been empirically supported. That is, while people's scores on personality tests do show changes over time to some extent, most psychologists attribute such changes mainly to weaknesses in the reliability of the tests—rather than to real changes in the individual's personality. Indeed, the consensus is that our "core" of attitudes, motivations, and behavioral tendencies shifts remarkably little as we go through daily life.

Not long ago, theorists suggested that major life events could significantly affect our personality: for instance, getting fired from a job might make us permanently more anxious or depressed, or becoming a parent might permanently raise our self-esteem. But more recent scientific evidence indicates that whenever we experience such upheavals, these are always mediated by our basic personality.

For example, imagine a commuter-train derailment disaster, in which a carload of people is badly injured. One person may leave the hospital utterly traumatized, afraid to travel or even work at all afterward. Another might experience the identical event as just a minor inconvenience, and quickly get back to normal activity. Still a third might view her hospitalization as an unexpected opportunity to see if health care is more interesting as a possible career than her entry-level accounting job.

In short, psychologists strongly agree that our personality remains stable throughout life and resists major change. In this light, many philosophers have suggested that people fear change more than any other aspect in everyday living; in the fields of counseling and psychotherapy, such "resistance," as it's called, has been recognized for a hundred years.

Have you ever heard the adage: "As people age, they become more intense versions of themselves"? In other words, an angry person becomes *angrier* as he or she gets older, an extravert becomes more outgoing, or a kindly individual becomes more altruistic. It sounds plausible, doesn't it? Well, at present there's no evidence that it holds true scientifically.

3. HOW IS PERSONALITY MEASURED?

The field of personality testing is close to a century old, but its basic features have been consistent. Whenever a test is constructed, it must meet several specific criteria scientifically, in particular, *reliability* and *validity*.

Reliability refers to the consistency of the results. Suppose a test seeks to measure how outgoing you are, and you just had a big, upsetting argument with your best friend. Could that event affect your performance, so that, for example, your test score shows you to be less gregarious than you normally are? Or suppose your mother was hospitalized yesterday for exploratory surgery. Could that elevate your score on a test designed to measure your normal degree of anxiety or depression?

Major personality tests do show significant reliability—and in an imperfect world, are accepted as worthwhile. But do these tests take such matters into account? The answer is no. I am aware of no personality tests that permit the individual to recount a problem or crisis that might be affecting his or her out-look, though an interview might certainly allow it.

The other major feature of tests is validity: Does the test actually measure what it seeks or claims to measure? This is probably the most challenging issue in current personality testing.

For instance, suppose a new test has been created to measure the trait of shyness. Immediately, psychologists start debating the issue: Does the test really measure shyness or does it inadvertently measure—at least to an extent—other traits, such as introversion or perhaps even depression? That is, maybe John or Allison is scoring high on this test not because of shyness, but because of a tendency to prefer solitude, or because of a depressed outlook.

In response, the test's defenders might argue: What do we mean by shyness anyway? Or introversion? Or even depression? Maybe they're all related in some way that social science doesn't yet fathom. Sound far-fetched to you? Confusing? Well, academic psychologists delight in focusing their time and energy on such matters. What does this tell you about *their* personality?

Finally, how is a personality test actually constructed? For example, how would we go about creating an instrument to identify those business students who would make successful entrepreneurs? While there might seem to be many ways to achieve this goal, most psychometricians today would do the following:

1. Establish a meaningful reference group; for instance, a sample of men and women who developed a business with profitability of $1 million or more during the first five years.

2. Conduct interviews with these entrepreneurs to identify their basic attitudes, interests, values, and motivations.

3. Distill these aspects into a series of items that can be placed in a personality inventory and answered in twenty to sixty minutes.

4. Further refine the items so that test scores can significantly differentiate among people: such as successful entrepreneurs versus those who failed in starting their own business.

5. Finally, psychometricians could assess predictive validity by giving the test to a group of one hundred MBA students, and then see whether scores will predict which of these will become successful entrepreneurs within five years of receiving their degrees.

In a nutshell, that is the method for test development.

Let's take another example. With increasing globalization in business today, there may be a real need for a test to identify those managers who could adapt most successfully to life in a foreign country. How would we construct such a test?

Here, of course, cultural issues become quite relevant. What makes for a successful adaptation for Germans or Swiss may be different from Japanese or

Canadians; yet, certain personality traits might be relevant for all, such as emotional flexibility, openness to change, and risk-taking ability.

What would be the criterion group? Suppose we're looking at American executives who adapt most successfully to working in London. We might interview business people who had lived as expatriates there for at least three years and described themselves as happy and content; then probe for their values, attitudes, motivations, expectations; next, develop a questionnaire of relevant items; and then, to measure the test's validity, give the test to a group of successful expatriates versus those who had quit their positions due to personal unhappiness. If the test is truly valid, there should be a statistically significant difference among the two groups.

Finally, to determine predictive validity, we might give the test to a group of potential expatriates and compare scores after a three-year period: Did the test distinguish significantly between the two groups?

Of course, for both tests in these two examples, psychometricians must also determine reliability. This can be done in various ways, such as administering the test to the same people twice in a six-month period and checking for consistency in their scores.

By now you should have a broad picture of personality study today. To understand your test-taking situation in the hiring process, it will also be helpful to know something about how the field has evolved.

3
Personality Testing: Then and Now

Reliance upon personality tests for hiring and promotion may be booming today, but it's a scientific field more than a century old. Understanding its history won't necessarily help you answer a specific item more effectively, but it will provide a valuable context for what workplace testing today is all about.

The field's founder was the eminent Sir Francis Galton of England, who in 1884 used a dictionary to show that human personality contains a specific number of groupable traits. For instance, words like "cheerful," "jovial," "merry," and "mirthful" comprise a quality embodying happy sociability, whereas "sad," "melancholy," and "gloomy" make up a different cluster. However, Galton's investigation was mainly theoretical and exerted little impact on business.

It was not until 1915 that personality study was put to major "real-world" usage, when the illustrious Carnegie Institute of Technology created a Division of Applied Psychology, and, the following year, a Bureau of Salesmanship Research. The bureau was established to sponsor research aimed on scientifically selecting salespeople by means of personality testing. It was in 1916, too, that the first American police department made use of psychological tests in the hiring process. Perhaps more than any other industry since, law enforcement has relied upon these instruments to identify suitable and unsuitable job candidates. After all, a hotheaded or impulsive salesperson may kill a lucrative deal, but a quick-tempered police officer may harm a real human being. As the latest newspaper headlines indicate, accurately pinpointing such potential misfits remains a vital social issue.

United States involvement in World War I greatly spurred the growth of psychological testing, for the military required measures that could be administered quickly to large groups of potential soldiers. These focused on intelligence and were the first of their kind to aid in personnel selection. With Robert Yerkes and John Otis among the key test developers, hundreds of thousands of recruits were evaluated with the Army Alpha (the main instrument) or the Army Beta, a nonverbal test for illiterates and nonnative English speakers.

The number of actual selection decisions that were based on these tests, however, remains unclear. Individual bases differed widely in their support for the testing enterprise and in their reliance on test results in screening and classifying recruits. Nevertheless, the massive amount of data collected by Yerkes and his colleagues heightened interest in using intelligence tests for selecting candidates in private industry.

Besides developing group tests of general intelligence, the U.S. Army during World War I originated a variety of so-called trade tests to measure specific job knowledge and skills. These were designed to separate the men tested into four groups of proficiency: (1) novices, (2) apprentices, (3) journeymen, and (4) experts. The tests themselves generally fell into three basic categories: verbal and picture tests—both using paper-and-pencil measurement of job knowledge—and performance tests, which generally involved "hands-on" use of job-related machinery.

Perhaps even more important, American involvement in World War I fostered the development of the first standardized personality test: the Woodworth Personal Data Sheet, also known as the Woodworth Test of Emotional Stability. During the war, the Woodworth Personal Data Sheet was administered to recruits for the purpose of screening for additional psychiatric examination—those recruits likely to "crack" during combat, and therefore unfit for military induction.

In 1919, after the war ended, the Committee on Classification of Personnel, associated with the U.S. Adjutant General's Office, began a program of personality data collection to help in deciding officer furloughs. Former employers' ratings of officer character traits—such as trustworthiness and leadership—were obtained and used as a decision tool.

Although personality tests during the First World War were chiefly used to identify recruits emotionally unfit for combat, professional interest in tests for predicting job performance grew rapidly. By the end of the war, for example, rating-scale methods of personality measurement—popularized by the military and by the Bureau of Salesmanship Research—were already being used by several personnel consulting firms and companies to predict job success.

Yet, most researchers knew that existing personality theory and methodology were still too primitive to create truly effective tests. As Yerkes observed in 1920, "Methods at once simple and reliable are not yet available. It is nevertheless obvious that personality attributes are as important as intelligence for industrial placement and vocational guidance." Yerkes and his colleagues were especially concerned about problems caused by the "halo effect," in which, for example, a well-liked employee is given inaccurately high ratings by his or her supervisor on aspects of job performance that have nothing to do with the actual "target" trait being measured—like conscientiousness or trustworthiness. This type of error is notorious in education, where teachers commonly give higher grades—especially on subjective tests like essays—to their favorite students.

During the 1920s and early 1930s an emphasis on improving test methodology brought several new paper-and-pencil personality measures to the workplace. Aimed at assessing specific traits, these included Gordon Allport's Ascendance-Submission Test (measuring self-esteem or dominance) and the Bernreuter Personality Inventory, which was an "all-in-one" measure of six scales that combined items from previously developed scales including Allport's.

In particular, the Bernreuter was found useful as a means for predicting the performance of salespeople, as well as those of nursing students and factory supervisors. Interestingly, however, managers found such tests disappointing in failing to identify those likely to emerge as either the best or the worst employees. As a result, many researchers advised caution in relying too heavily on psychological tests in making hiring choices.

The 1940s witnessed the appearance of the Minnesota Multiphasic Personality Inventory (MMPI) as a leading personality test, encompassing over five hundred questions and a variety of subscales, including a special "lying" scale to determine if the job applicant was grossly inflating his or her personality strengths. During World War II the Cornell Science Index provided the equivalent of the Woodworth Personal Data Sheet to screen out emotionally unstable recruits.

In that period, the use of personality testing in the workplace grew steadily. For example, the Life Insurance Sales Research Bureau sought to assess specific personality traits related to performance by life insurance salespeople; such traits as self-confidence were assessed in combination with a personal history measure. In another series of studies, the bureau explored the personality traits seemingly linked to successful salesmanship. Likewise in the 1940s, the Sears company commissioned psychologist Robert Thurstone to develop a procedure for selecting executives. The resulting test battery included the Guilford Martin Personality Inventories—revised in 1949 as the Guilford and Zimmerman Temperament Survey—as well as ability and interest measures. Sears screened more than ten thousand people by means of such personality tests.

The entry of the United States into World War II greatly accelerated the growth of standardized testing. Many prominent psychologists, as well as those who would gain prominence in the postwar years, worked hard together in helping to defeat Nazi Germany. They developed ability tests to select and classify thousands of military personnel in the Army, Navy, Army Air Force, and the Office of Strategic Services (OSS). Never before had it been feasible to so rapidly move through cycles of job analysis, creation of ability tests, evaluation of test validity and reliability, and refinement of procedures. It's hardly surprising, therefore, that so much progress was made in both the methodology and application of testing.

Indeed, World War II proved a watershed in legitimizing the use of psychological tests in the workplace. Managers and executives affirmed their value, and surveys showed that by the mid-1950s nearly two-thirds of large companies were using personality and interest tests in employee selection. Yet, many academicians expressed caution about the worth of such measures. For one thing, a proliferation of tests due to organizational needs created many instruments of dubious reliability and validity. While these seemed to satisfy organizational objectives, most rested on meager theory. Likewise, academicians also voiced concern about the use of tests like the MMPI in predicting employee productivity or achievement, rather than in merely screening for emotional stability. Typically, psychologists insisted that there was too little scientific data to justify such empirical leaps; as two prominent researchers insisted in 1965, "The best that can be said is that in some situations, for some purposes, some personality measures can offer helpful predictions."

By the advent of President Lyndon Johnson's "Great Society" legislative program of the mid-1960s, the use of personality tests in employee selection had reached unprecedented levels. But organizational enthusiasm for psychological testing suddenly began to wane due to a barrage of criticism that such tests were racially and ethnically discriminatory, unreliable, and easily faked. The Civil Rights Act of 1964, the establishment of the Equal Employment Opportunity Commission (EEOC), and subsequent landmark U.S. Supreme Court rulings laid out the circumstances under which the use of testing for personnel selection would be allowed, and the nature of validation evidence that firms would be required to prove in the event of a legal challenge to the use of a test. Fearing long and expansive legal challenges, many companies immediately began reducing their use of personality tests in favor of other techniques, like interviews.

As a result, the use of personality testing in business declined sharply for all but the most sensitive positions, such as police officers, air traffic controllers, and nuclear plant operators. For these types of jobs, personality tests like the MMPI continued to be used in employee screening.

During this same period, personality testing also came under attack from psychological theorists. Though new instruments like the Myers-Briggs Type Scale (based on psychiatrist Carl Jung's theory of personality types) came into vogue, and renowned thinkers like Abraham Maslow advocated more extensive types of assessment, including efforts to uncover employees' "higher" needs and motivations, others condemned the whole field as misguided—and even questioned whether we really have stable, enduring personalities at all. As a graduate student at the University of Michigan in those days, I can well recall the obvious absurdity of such arguments.

In the 1970s personality testing hit the doldrums, and the whole notion of using tests to screen job applicants went on the defensive. But a rebound was inevitable, and slowly a new model for understanding human personality began to emerge. It coalesced on a five-factor approach, which argued that virtually all normal adult personality could be understood in terms of five overall dimensions: Extraversion, Conscientiousness, Neuroticism, Agreeableness, and Openness to Experience.

Ironically, by focusing on human personality in terms of commonly used adjectives like "outgoing," "diligent," "moody," "amiable," and "artistic," the

Big Five model—as it's come to be known—strongly follows the outlook of Sir Francis Galton, who pioneered the field of personality study a century ago. Perhaps predictably, perhaps not, we've definitely come full circle back to the starting point of thinking about our inner world.

Not only has the Big Five model proven appealing to theorists, it has also generated a large amount of empirical research showing its usefulness in many settings, including the workplace. For instance, psychologists have found the Big Five model to be helpful in predicting those who will benefit most from counseling, as well as those who will exhibit greatest on-the-job competence. A variety of studies have demonstrated, too, that the Big Five approach is valid for assessing people in widely different cultures, such as China, India, Japan, the Philippines, and South America. Interestingly, there's evidence that Asians have a sixth major component of normal adult personality not found frequently among Occidentals, which researchers call "filial piety." This is a trait involving dutiful feelings and behaviors toward one's parents and other respected elders, and which is separate from the other five personality dimensions.

The Big Five approach, of course, has its critics. Some psychologists have argued that none of the five scales measure such important qualities as creativity, innovativeness, or the ability to resist conformity. Others have insisted that the Big Five model lacks a scale of spirituality or self-transcendence—values highly meaningful for some people's lives, and which may well be biologically or genetically mediated.

Nevertheless, the Big Five model has become so popular and influential that it now dominates the field of personality testing. As a result, you're likely to be tested in most job screenings on at least two of its major scales—extraversion and conscientiousness—as well as, perhaps, neuroticism and agreeableness.

In this book you'll gain a great deal of practice in responding to items that reflect these personality constructs. You'll also become proficient in handling tests that focus on integrity/honesty, proneness to anger, stress tolerance, entrepreneurialism, and leadership. Such personality aspects are frequently assessed by human resource managers today, and you'd be wise to master their underlying concepts and test questions. Because personality is still assessed in many work settings by means of a semistructured job interview, I've also included a chapter that will help prepare you for that often anxiety-producing situation.

The field of personality assessment has never been static, and undoubtedly the new millennium will see additional change. By all indicators, such testing will only increase in importance through the coming years. So in managing your career advancement, the more you know about personality testing, the greater likelihood of your success.

4
Mental Probing
by Interview

Though personality tests have become increasingly prevalent, formal interviews are still a vital feature of the selection process. And inevitably, they're stressful situations for job candidates. It's a truism in the human resource field that interviews are often unreliable, possess doubtful validity, and provide little useful information to guide employers in hiring effectively. Yet, interviews are deemed essential for almost all managerial and professional positions. Go figure.

One reason, of course, is that résumés and letters of recommendation are notoriously unreliable. Not only do many people embellish the truth about their specific job history or college education, but some utterly fabricate even the names of their former employers or alma maters. In fact, an entire industry has arisen in recent years devoted just to verifying whether a job candidate actually attended Cornell or worked for five years at IBM. Likewise, letters of recommendation are well-known to be filled with half-truths, if not wild exaggerations; after all, what are best friends for? Also, due to the fear of retaliatory lawsuits, many organizations today refuse to provide reference letters concerning their workers and will identify only their job titles and period of employment. As a result of such factors, personality interviewing remains very much with us.

It's a truism that interviews can only *lose* the job for candidates, but almost never *gain* them the job. Why? Because, in a sense, the employment interview is a highly unnatural, artificial, and contrived situation—totally unlike almost all others we experience in ordinary life. When all the subtleties are stripped away, be aware that it's a *screening* to ensure that the candidate is emotionally stable, cooperative, reasonably pleasant, and verbally responsive.

Besides being inappropriately dressed or groomed, you can blow an interview by losing your cool and answering a tricky question the wrong way, even if you're obviously being honest, innocuous, and even helpful. We may be living in a new millennium, but surprisingly, there are still many employers who will categorically refuse to hire a candidate who mentions having been in personal counseling or therapy.

Indeed, my friend Jeff in New York City recently discovered this truth the hard way. Personable and well-qualified, he was at the interview stage of the hiring process for a prestigious administrative position. All was going beautifully, and the coveted job seemed within Jeff's easy grasp. But then, in response to a personality probe, he casually mentioned that therapy was helping him to strike a better balance between work and family. To Jeff's utter shock, the interview was abruptly terminated moments later, and he never got the job. Not only do many interviewers not want to hear about the candidate's need to "balance" work with anything else, but to learn of his or her psychotherapy is a sure kiss of death.

Here are twenty-one typical, open-ended questions designed to guide interviewers in uncovering your personality. Some come directly from recent articles aimed at helping human resource professionals separate the proverbial wheat from the chaff. Although you may not be asked them all, it's likely that several will pop up at you. First, answer each question on a sheet of paper as accurately as you can. Then see what interviewers actually want to hear in order to hire the stranger sitting warily before them.

Open-Ended Questions that Probe for Honesty/Integrity

1. Describe an event in your life when your integrity was challenged at work. How did you deal with it?

2. How would you handle it if someone at work asked you to do something you felt was unethical?

3. Have you ever experienced a lapse in judgment about doing what was right?

4. In what business situations do you feel that honesty would *not* be advisable?

5. Have you ever seen a coworker doing something dishonest at work? If so, did you tell your boss? Why or why not?

General Open-Ended Questions

6. In your life, what motivates you the most?

7. What would you say is your greatest personal weakness?

8. How would your best friends describe your personality?

9. How would you describe yourself?

10. What gives you the greatest sense of fulfillment at work?

11. Describe a work situation in which you felt very frustrated.

12. What kinds of people do you most enjoy working with, and why?

13. What kinds of people do you prefer *not* to work with, and why?

14. What kind of work setting do you like the most, and why?

15. What kind of work setting do you like the least, and why?

16. Have you ever had a conflict with a coworker? If so, how did you attempt to resolve the conflict? Were you successful? Why or why not?

17. How would you describe your management style? If your subordinates had to describe you in three words, what would those words be?

18. Tell me about the best teacher who you ever had, in school or college. Now tell me about the worst teacher, either in school or college.

19. Have you ever made an enemy at work? If so, why do you think that happened? Do you think it could happen again?

20. What do you think employees owe to their employer? What does an employer owe to its employees?

21. Name three well-known people who you most admire for their leadership ability.

ANALYSIS OF PROBE QUESTIONS

Open-Ended Questions that Probe for Honesty/Integrity

1. Describe an event in your life when your integrity was challenged at work. How did you deal with it?

    For such a question, you should be prepared to recall in fairly substantial detail an actual event from your life. Of course, you should describe an event in which you showed conviction and integrity, and never wavered about the right course of action. Do not describe an event in which you wavered, even for an instant, in doing the ethical thing—or worse, in which you showed poor judgment or poor integrity.

2. How would you handle it if someone at work asked you to do something you felt was unethical?

    For all such hypothetical questions, it is wise to give a strong, decisive answer: namely, that you would never, under any circumstances, agree to do something unethical. Adding that you would quickly report the request to your supervisor is also worthwhile.

3. Have you ever experienced a lapse in judgment about doing what was right?

    Of course, the wise response is that you have never experienced a laps' in judgment about doing what was right, because your ethical system is s important in your daily life.

4. In what business situations do you feel that honesty would *not* be advisab

The appropriate response is that honesty is necessary in all business situations, and that it is never inadvisable. You can talk for a few minutes that in the long run, only honest conduct prevails, and that liars and crooks almost always get caught in the end. You can cite our illustrious Founding Father Ben Franklin, who sagaciously declared, "Honesty is the best policy."

5. Have you ever seen a coworker doing something dishonest at work? If so, did you tell your boss? Why or why not?

It is wise to answer that you have never seen a coworker doing something dishonest, but that if you did, you would not hesitate to report it immediately to your supervisor. You might add that you have zero tolerance for dishonesty at work, and believe that companies should have zero tolerance, too.

General Open-Ended Questions

6. In your life, what motivates you the most?

It's appropriate to say that working hard to accomplish goals and experiencing that wonderful feeling of satisfaction from a job well done are your greatest motivators. You can give a specific example about a challenge, such as a completed work assignment, that you feel good about.

7. What would you say is your greatest personal weakness?

Beware of this question! It has ruined more candidates than will ever be known. You can respond that you have no real weaknesses you're aware of; or, that your only real weakness is that you tend to push yourself too hard sometimes at work. If you have any real emotional weaknesses—even seemingly trivial ones like fear of heights, fear of dogs, or occasional difficulty in falling asleep at night—now isn't the time to "share." Trust me.

8. How would your best friends describe your personality?

Of course, your best friends would describe you as honest, trustworthy, outgoing, and conscientious, someone who takes work seriously—maybe who even works a little too hard. You can add a socially acceptable hobby, preferably a sport, like golf or tennis. Mentioning more intellectual pursuits like chess or solving Latin crossword puzzles is dicey, as is describing offbeat interests like collecting bottlecaps from Balkan countries or Vietnam War memorabilia. Remember, do not present yourself as too unconventional.

9. How would you describe yourself?

By now you should have the basic idea. You should describe yourself as hardworking, conscientious, someone who takes every task seriously, who enjoys the feeling of accomplishment and is always a team player.

10. What gives you the greatest sense of fulfillment at work?

    An appropriate response is that, certainly, what gives you the greatest sense of fulfillment at work is seeing a job through to completion—and knowing that you're part of a team working for the good of the organization.

11. Describe a work situation where you felt very frustrated.

    A wise answer is that you honestly can't recall a situation at work that really frustrated you. Explain that you definitely know that work often produces stress, and that you handle it well. You can admit to getting a bit frustrated, however, if you're not allowed to finish a job that you start because of changing priorities in the organization. But then add that, as a team player, you accept that such things happen.

12. What kinds of people do you most enjoy working with, and why?

    It's wise to answer that you most enjoy working with people like yourself: that is, who take their work very seriously, who apply themselves conscientiously, and who love the feeling of accomplishment for a job well done. You can add that you seem to meet many fine people like that from your experience at work.

13. What kinds of people do you prefer *not* to work with, and why?

    Be consistent with your response to question number 12. That is, you prefer *not* to work with people who don't take their job seriously, who like to goof off, fool around, or do as little as possible on the job: in short, people who don't value that marvelous feeling of accomplishment from a job well done. You can add that you've been fortunate in not having had to work alongside many people like that.

14. What kind of work setting do you like the most, and why?

    It's smart to reply that work settings don't matter all that much to you. The important thing is to get the job done. In two relevant phrases, you're flexible and adapt well to different settings. Next question?

15. What kind of work setting do you like the least, and why?

    Remember the tone of your response to question number 14. To be consistent, you ought to indicate that no particular work setting bothers you, that you function well in many different types of settings. You might add that, after all, you're a very flexible and adaptable person.

16. Have you ever had a conflict with a coworker? If so, how did you attempt to resolve the conflict? Were you successful? Why or why not?

    It's appropriate to say that you can't recall ever having had a major conflict with a coworker. But if such a conflict ever arises, you would certainly be flexible and accommodating, and focus on seeing the issue from your coworker's viewpoint. You might add that when people look at disagreements in this way, successful compromises almost always occur.

17. How would you describe your management style? If your subordinates had to describe you in three words, what would those words be?

   It's wise to say that your management style is one of being structured, giving assignments clearly, making frequent follow-ups but in a supportive way, and indicating that you take deadlines seriously and expect people to give a hundred percent commitment to their work. Three words? Organized, conscientious, and supportive. Here are a few more for good luck: reliable, dependable, team-player.

18. Tell me about the best teacher you ever had, in school or college. Now tell me about the worst teacher, also either in school or college.

   It's helpful if you can describe an actual teacher who inspired you. But if not, put together a composite. Your best teacher was hardworking, took the subject seriously but also had a sense of humor, and motivated nearly all of his or her students to strive and excel. You can add that come to think of it, that's your philosophy about work too.

   It's appropriate to reply that you've been fortunate in not having any really "bad" teachers. But it's all right to say that some didn't seem to be very diligent in lesson planning or evaluating student homework, and these teachers transmitted that indifferent, lackadaisical attitude to their students. In your view, that's not good at all.

19. Have you ever made an enemy at work? If so, why do you think that happened? Do you think it could happen again?

   You'd be an idiot to say that you've made enemies at work. Of course you've never made an enemy at work, and in fact you've gotten along very well with your coworkers. It must be because you've applied yourself very hard, taken your job seriously, and always been a team player. And, when the situation called for it, you were willing to go "the extra mile" for the good of the organization.

20. What do you think employees owe to their employer? What does an employer owe to its employees?

   It's wise to answer that employees owe their employer a hundred percent commitment of motivation and effort. Also, to work hard, to see tasks through to completion, and to be a team player. As for the employer, it's important to treat employees fairly, and to let them know what is expected in terms of their specific job responsibilities.

21. Name three people who you most admire for their leadership ability.

   Here, you can certainly be sincere, as long as your choices are fairly conventional. Mentioning highly successful CEOs and entrepreneurs is your safest bet—people like Bill Gates, Steven Jobs, and Katharine Graham of the *Washington Post.* Wax eloquent about their long-range vision, sense of mission, perseverance, and their ability to excite others through such qualities. You can also throw in a creative type like Steven Spielberg, Bill Cosby, or Oprah Winfrey. In your answer, stay away from naming particular politicians, and ditto for religious leaders. Bad choices definitely include the Unabomber and Saddam Hussein.

Well, now, that was a lot easier than you thought, wasn't it?

5
Mastering the Test-Taking Procedure

Personality tests often have different features, but they share many commonalities. It's therefore helpful to gain familiarity with the basic elements of test-taking before you're involved with the real-life situation. For one thing, you'll feel a lot calmer—and more confident—knowing what to expect. You'll also be less likely to get confused and make errors that can only hurt you during the testing procedure.

Here are eight important pointers to guide you:

1. Typically, Personality Tests Are Timed.

You'll be given enough time to answer all questions, but you'll need to respond quickly and efficiently. Forget about the luxury of leisurely musing or meticulous analyzing your way through it. At most, you'll have about a half minute per question. This means you'll be given approximately an hour to complete a 100-item test. Yes, you'll find it a high-pressure experience.

2. There's Definitely a "Right" Response to Every Question, No Matter What the Test Instructions May Say.

Indeed, the whole purpose of this book is help you determine what the test is really trying to discover about you. In some cases even a few "wrong" answers on a personality test can eliminate you from job consideration.

3. Think Before You Respond.

The test's instructions may specifically advise you not to mull over your answer, but that's exactly what's necessary to appear your best. Sometimes, an item may be worded in a tricky or obscure manner, and you may definitely have to read it a few times until its meaning is clear. In fact, you can expect to find many questions that require rereading, often because psychologists use wording in the double negative: for example, "I never find it hard to fall asleep at night" or "I have never been accused of dishonesty at work." Do *not* answer a question until you're certain of its meaning.

4. Almost All Personality Tests Use a Five-point Scale, or Occasionally, a Seven-point Scale.

Known as Likert-type scales for their founder, psychologist Renee Likert, these present a statement, such as, "I am considered a very happy person," and then offer five or seven possible responses: *strongly disagree, disagree, neutral, agree,* and *strongly agree;* or else, *very strongly disagree, strongly disagree, neutral, agree, strongly agree,* and *very strongly agree.*

You must mark only one as your response. Generally, it's best to avoid checking off the *neutral* category, which indicates that you lack strong feelings either way about the question. Why? Because in virtually all situations, the test's creators and administrators are looking for strong responses—either agreement or disagreement, depending on how the item is worded. After all, would *you* hire someone who didn't seem to care about workplace violence, theft, or leadership?

How do you determine if you *agree* versus *strongly agree* with a particular statement? Or, if you *disagree* versus *strongly disagree?* It may seem unfair, but the distinction is sometimes arbitrary, and sometimes not. By the time you've completed this book's varied practice tests, you'll have a much better sense of which category is most desirable from the test creator's viewpoint. Example: If you're being asked about how extraverted (outgoing) you are, it's better to *strongly agree* than merely *agree* with a statement like, "I enjoy loud parties." Conversely, it's better to *strongly disagree* than merely *disagree* with a statement such as, "Most people steal at work."

In the past, some personality tests were designed to screen out people who checked off too frequently the extreme end points of a scale: that is, *strongly disagree/strongly agree* in a five-point scale, or *very strongly disagree/very strongly agree* in a seven-point scale. The psychologists' attitude was that such people are "extremists" and likely to be over-opinionated or even hotheaded in their views. No longer do psychologists take this position; still, you never know what obsolete scoring may still be used in the test you take.

For this reason it's desirable to check off at least a few non-"extreme" categories, even when responding to questions on workplace honesty or anger, where you're *supposed* to have sharp, decisive views.

5. Be Sure to Answer All Test Questions.

Almost inevitably, you're going to encounter some questions that seem strange, silly, or just plain poorly-worded. Hey, psychologists are human, too. Avoid the temptation to skip such a seemingly pointless question. Job candidates who omit too many items are likely to have their tests invalidated and be dropped from consideration. You don't want that to happen, so just reread the question until it becomes coherent. If you're still unclear about its meaning, then check off the *neutral* category.

6. Almost All Personality Tests Contain a Built-in "Lie" Scale, Which Is Designed to Indicate If a Candidate Is Obviously Faking His or Her Answers.

Those who score above the cutoff on the "lie" scale will almost certainly have their test results invalidated and be removed from job consideration. Chapter Six specifically coaches you on how to field such "softball" questions as, "I have never hurt anyone's feelings" or "I have never told a lie." It may surprise you, but candidates indeed fail personality tests because of their elevated scores on the "lie" scale.

7. Don't Erase Unless You Absolutely Must.

Again, this means that you ought not to answer impulsively. Read the question carefully a few times before responding. If you're taking a paper-and-pencil test rather than one via computer and the Internet, your erasures may not be accurately detected. Of course, make sure you erase in a clean manner.

8. Finally, Don't Play Amateur Psychologist or Try to "Second-guess" the Test's Creator.

Remember, personality assessment in the workplace is a big business aimed solely at determining which candidates are most likely to perform well on the job. The seven types of traits highlighted in this book—conscientiousness, extraversion, anger, integrity, entrepreneurialism, stress, and leadership—are essentially what most employers are trying to uncover about you. Other qualities, such as your closeness to relatives, political involvement, religious convictions, or sexual proclivities, are not only irrelevant to this goal, but are often outside legal bounds as well. So don't look for a "hidden agenda."

If you master the information presented here and take the sample tests diligently, there's virtually no need to try second-guessing the test, especially during the stress of actually taking the examination.

6

The Lie Scale: Fielding "Softball" Questions

Before we get to specific aspects of personality assessment, it's important to know that almost all tests you're likely to take contain what I call "softball" questions because they're actually so easy to handle. These are essentially "trick" items that are included to see if you are trying to fool the tester by pretending to be emotionally more stable, vibrant, and attractive than you really are.

So definitely beware of the following types of questions. They're aimed at determining if you're responding honestly to the test. Be especially wary of questions that contain the words "always," "all the time," and "never." These words are tip-offs for the presence of a softball coming straight at you.

Remember, you're not expected to be a perfect human being or a saint. By the way, you *are* expected to be completely honest and trustworthy, as well as a zero risk for workplace violence, but those are subjects for later chapters.

Claiming to be infallible, or the most wonderful person on earth, or omniscient, is not advisable. If you exceed the point limit on the "lie" scale of a particular personality test, all your results are considered suspicious and your entire test will most likely be thrown out. The probability of your being hired for the position will immediately diminish to near zero. Believe it or not, sometimes even a couple of "lying" responses will place a candidate's test results and job application in the human resource department's gray category, rather than its white category for *definitely hire*.

Example 1. Everything I Do Is Interesting to Me.

Note the word *everything*. Nobody on this planet, not even the President of the United States, or your favorite famous athlete, movie star, or big-name entertainer can legitimately claim this statement to be true. No company expects you to find every aspect of work—or life, for that matter—to be interesting.

Therefore, stay away from either the *agree* or *strongly agree* responses for this type of question. On a five-point measure, you'd be wise to indicate a 2—that you *moderately disagree* with this statement.

Example 2. I Have Never Told a Lie.

Note the word *never*. Not even George Washington or "Honest Abe" Lincoln could validly claim this statement to be accurate. To insist that you've never lied in your life is obviously ridiculous. On a five-point measure, if you indicate either agreement or strong agreement with this statement, you're therefore going to trip a resounding alarm on the "lie scale."

Instead, you'd be smart to indicate a *1* for *strongly disagree.*

Example 3. I Have Never Actually Lost My Temper.

The newspapers and magazines today are filled with articles about rage. There's road rage, air rage, and certainly employee rage—known as "going postal," about which we'll focus later in this book. Workplace violence and sabotage are major concerns nowadays to employers, and they're increasingly turning to professionally designed personality tests to screen out potential hotheads, misfits, and troublemakers.

But everybody has lost their temper at least occasionally. How about the time as a kid when you didn't get that birthday or Christmas present you desperately wanted? Or when you were badly overcharged for a repair service? Remember, you're not presenting yourself as an android or alien being.

If you mark *agree*—or, God help you—*strongly agree* with this statement, the lie scale's alarm is definitely going to start resounding. Rather, the sensible response is to *moderately disagree;* so, on a five-point measure, a 2 is most appropriate.

Get the idea? Answer each of the following sixty-eight questions in such a manner so as to keep that alarm from going off.

1. I have never failed to reach a personal goal I set for myself.
2. I have planned ahead in everything I've done.
3. I have never hurt anyone's feelings.
4. I never question my decisions after I make them.
5. I have never made a statement that was not completely true.
6. I always finish what I start.
7. I have never talked about someone behind his or her back.
8. I have never found loose change on the street and kept it.
9. I have never been bored.
10. I follow through on everything I ever do.
11. I have never disappointed anyone.
12. I have never failed to complete a school or work assignment on time.
13. I have never lost a friend.

14. I have never made a mistake at work.

15. I have never driven a car above the posted speed limit.

16. At a party, I have never said the wrong thing to anybody.

17. I have never lost a night's sleep worrying about something.

18. I have never felt angry at a supervisor or boss.

19. I have never been annoyed with a coworker.

20. I always leave my work-area spotless at the end of the workday.

21. All my work has been appreciated and valued by others.

22. I have never felt tired at the end of a workday.

23. No work assignment has ever bored me.

24. I always find meetings to be interesting at work.

25. I have never been late for anything.

26. I have never gotten to work late.

27. I have never become impatient while waiting on a line in the post office or supermarket.

28. Most people who know me would agree that I have no faults.

29. I have never acted on an impulse.

30. I have never read a boring book.

31. I have never sat through a dull movie.

32. People who know me usually describe me as fascinating.

33. I have a large number of interesting hobbies.

34. As a student, I excelled in everything.

35. I have never refused to help someone who asked me.

36. While growing up, I never had a tantrum.

37. I never disliked a teacher.

38. I have never argued with a parent.

39. I have never actually been lost.

40. I never missed a schoolday or workday because of illness.

41. I have always had great admiration for my bosses and supervisors.

42. I have always had the perfect job.

43. I have never been tired at work.

44. I have never paid a bill late or not at all.

45. My last boss or supervisor had no faults that I can recall.

46. I have never felt like leaving a party.

47. I have never been overcharged in a restaurant.

48. I have never had a bad haircut.

49. I have never been a bad sport after an athletic game.

50. Most people would describe me as charming to know.

51. I am extremely graceful.

52. I have never been rude to anyone.

53. I have never complained about service at a restaurant.

54. I have gotten along perfectly with every coworker I've ever had.

55. I am always full of energy.

56. I have never forgotten where I put something.

57. I've been a success at everything I've ever tried.

58. I am always happy.

59. I have never felt sad.

60. I have never felt alone.

61. I have never been disappointed by anything.

62. I am a superb athlete.

63. People always describe me as having a terrific personality.

64. I have never had a cold.

65. I have never had a headache.

66. I have never used bad language to anyone.

67. I am admired by everyone who has ever met me.

68. I have never met someone I didn't like.

By now you should be able to field a "softball" question whenever it appears on a workplace personality test and recognize its presence as an alarm bell for lying. Armed with this knowledge, you're ready to focus on the seven key dimensions of assessment.

PART 2
Specific Realms of Assessment

7

Conscientiousness: Can You Be Absolutely Counted On?

The most important predictor of job performance has been identified as *conscientiousness.* Know well: This is a distinct personality trait. There are plenty of smart people who lack it, as do numerous men and women with great personalities. Maybe in the new global workplace the rules for financial investment have totally changed, but in all companies—high-tech, low-tech, and in between—*conscientious* employees are eagerly sought and valued. Nobody loves a slacker. Nobody wants a slacker.

Certainly, while it overlaps with other work-related qualities, *conscientiousness* is measurably different. Psychologists have been successful in developing various types of questions that help to identify a candidate's capability in this vital domain. Surprisingly, it's a relatively new construct, one that didn't exist independently even a generation ago. However, its closest, oldest "cousin" was known as "achievement motivation."

Like all other personality traits, *conscientiousness* is understood as encompassing several aspects, such as:

1. feeling competent about oneself
2. being orderly and tidy
3. being dutiful—that is, respectful of supervisors and accepting of prescribed routines
4. striving to achieve goals
5. having adequate self-discipline
6. being deliberate rather than impulsive

Does this sound like you? If so, whether through the luck of genetics or effective parenting—the "jury" is still out on this trait's roots, so take your pick—you will earn high job ratings on *conscientiousness* from future supervisors. If those features seem to be describing someone not at all like you, then you may be perceived as a goof-off. And, contrary to some recent Hollywood comedies, goof-offs rarely get promoted or placed into creative new jobs where they meet exciting and dynamic people bristling with success.

Can you learn to be more conscientious if that's not your natural bent? The psychological evidence moderately suggests yes, though such major traits don't change overnight and don't change without a lot of practice and effort. So the choice is yours.

Before tackling the sample personality tests that focus on conscientiousness, here are the three hiring zones that emanate from testing, and which, for job recruiters, decisively differentiate among candidates:

Definitely Hire:

This person is logical, careful, resourceful, and well-prepared. She is tidy, punctual, well-organized, and follows her ethical principles. She seeks to be highly successful and to perform an excellent job in whatever she undertakes. She has strong determination, persistence, and the ability to force herself to accomplish her goals. She is methodical and prudent.

Maybe Hire:

This person is usually logical, well-prepared, and well-organized. She is not always punctual; nor does she consistently follow her ethical principles. She seeks to be successful, but does not have the capacity to force herself to accomplish her goals. She strives for excellence, and has relatively high determination, but lacks persistence and is sometimes imprudent and unmethodical.

Definitely Do Not Hire:

This person is illogical, careless, and impulsive. She is poorly organized and does not follow her own ethical principles. She is sloppy, untidy, and unmotivated to try her best. She is lazy, weak-willed, and gives up easily when challenged. She does not force herself to accomplish significant goals. She is haphazard, hasty, and impetuous.

Sample Test Questions:

It's a sure bet that any psychological test you take for hiring will have questions that measure your conscientiousness. To help you focus clearly on this key trait, three sample tests with items that assess only conscientiousness will follow. Be aware, though, that these kinds of questions are typically interspersed through-out the overall personality test you'll be taking and will definitely not appear consecutively.

CONSCIENTIOUSNESS TEST #1

1. I love the feeling of a "job well done."

2. In my opinion, a job that isn't done perfectly isn't really done.

3. The most successful people are those who always complete what they begin.

   You want to strongly agree with this sort of statement in order to show your conscientiousness. Your role models should be those who finish whatever they start.

4. It's unreasonable to think that every job can be completed on time.

5. Sometimes, it's okay to leave a job unfinished if you know that a coworker will end up finishing it well.

6. I have almost never forgotten to show up for an appointment.

   This sort of question probes for your reliability, so a strongly agree response is desirable.

7. Employees should generally be expected to work extra hours to finish a job on time.

8. I know many people who work themselves too hard.

   On personality tests for hiring, there's nothing more valued than hard work, and workaholics don't exist. A strongly disagree response is therefore advised.

9. I admire people who put in long hours at work.

10. It's important to balance work with leisure interests and activities.

11. People who know me sometimes say I work too hard.

12. It's important for me to feel productive at work.

13. Americans should have more paid vacation days, as Europeans do.

14. Vacations are important to me for rest and relaxation.

15. I feel sorry for people who put in long hours at work.

    Employers expect their hires these days to work more hours than ever before. So you certainly want to strongly disagree with this sort of statement.

16. People who know me often call me a "team player."

> *In today's workplace, there are few traits*
> *more highly prized than teamwork or*
> *cooperativeness. So, of course, you want to*
> *strongly agree with such statements.*

17. Being part of a team is basic to most jobs today.

18. I would avoid hiring someone who didn't seem to be a "team player."

19. I try to keep my lunch breaks as short as possible so I can be most productive at work.

20. If I have to work late, or on a weekend, I usually don't mind.

21. The most productive employees are those who focus on their job regardless of how long it takes.

22. Many people foolishly sacrifice their personal lives for work success.

23. Work can be an addiction just like gambling or alcohol.

> *For today's time-pressed managers, all*
> *comments about "work-as-addiction" rub*
> *the wrong way. Definitely respond with a*
> *disagree or strongly disagree.*

24. I have never been called a "workaholic."

25. I admire people who are orderly and tidy at work.

26. Work is the most important thing in my life.

> *It's okay to affirm a hobby like tennis or golf*
> *as a way to unwind, but managers want to*
> *hear that work comes first in your life. So*
> *agree is a recommended response.*

27. It's unrealistic to expect an employee to work hard every single day.

28. People who know me describe me as very dependable when it comes to keeping appointments.

29. Some workdays, I have a lot of difficulty getting started.

30. I envy people who can take early retirement from work.

CONSCIENTIOUSNESS TEST #2

1. The feeling of a "job well done" is overrated.

2. It's not true that every job should be done perfectly.

3. At work, I don't always finish what I start.

4. Sometimes very successful people fail to finish what they start.

5. I'm not bothered by employees who leave jobs undone.

6. It's not unreasonable to think that every job should be completed on time.

7. It's wrong to leave a job unfinished if you know that a coworker will end up finishing it well.

8. People should be exacting when it comes to keeping appointments.

9. Employees should not generally be expected to work extra hours to finish a job on time.

> *A sign of your conscientiousness is precisely your willingness to work additional hours. So strongly disagree is an advisable response.*

10. I don't think many people in our society work too hard.

11. I don't admire people who put in long hours at work.

12. It's not important to balance work with leisure interests and activities.

13. People who know me never say I work too hard.

> *On these kinds of personality tests, the best weakness to admit is a tendency to overwork. So, it's worthwhile to respond with a disagree.*

14. If someone expects me to do something, I sometimes forget to do it.

15. A lot of the people I know could be called "workaholics."

16. Americans have enough paid vacation days.

17. Vacations are not important to me for rest and relaxation. ·

18. I don't feel sorry for people who put in long hours at work.

19. People who know me rarely call me a "team player."

20. Being part of a team isn't basic to most jobs today.

21. I would hire someone who didn't seem to be a "team player."

22. I never envy people whose jobs allow them long lunch breaks at a nice restaurant.

23. If I have to work late, or on a weekend, I usually feel bothered a little.

> *Remember, you want to present yourself as someone who does whatever is necessary to complete a task. So it's advisable to disagree or strongly disagree with this item.*

24. It's silly to say that work can be an addiction just like gambling or alcohol.

25. It's not important for me to be orderly and tidy at work.

26. Work is not very important in my life.

27. It's not unrealistic to expect an employee to work hard every single day.

> *Certainly, managers expect their employers to work hard every day, at least as a goal. So it's advisable to strongly agree with this statement.*

28. I am not considered a very dependable person in keeping appointments.

29. People who know me do not consider me very reliable about finishing what I start.

30. If I didn't need the money, I don't think I would always work to keep busy and productive.

> *This item is a bit tricky. Managers recognize that money is a key motivator for most employees, but on these tests it's generally better to affirm "higher" values like the satisfaction of a job well done. A worthwhile answer would be disagree.*

CONSCIENTIOUSNESS TEST #3

1. I love the feeling of completing a job well.

2. In my view, every job should be done perfectly.

3. I've sometimes been called a perfectionist at work.

4. Sometimes, it's okay to leave a job unfinished if you know that another employee will finish it well.

5. I can't recall ever forgetting to show up for an appointment.

6. Every employee should be expected to work extra hours to finish a job on time.

7. I think our society has too many people who are working too hard.

8. It's necessary for people to balance work with leisure interests and activities.

9. People who know me usually say I work too hard.

10. If someone at work expects me to do something, I can't say that I always do it.

11. It's very important for me to feel useful at work.

12. Americans should have more paid vacation days, like workers in other countries.

13. I value my vacation time a lot.

*Sorry to inform you, but managers don't want
to hear about your vacation preferences,
plans, or fantasies. You'd be wise to
strongly disagree with this statement.*

14. People who know me always call me a "team player."

15. Being part of a team is essential for most jobs today.

16. I would never hire someone who didn't seem to be a "team player."

17. Often I'd like to have a long lunch break at a nice restaurant to break the pressure of work.

18. If I have to work late, or on a weekend, I never mind.

19. The most productive employees are those who focus on their job regardless of how long it takes.

20. Work can certainly become addictive, like gambling or alcohol.

21. I dislike people who seem to be "workaholics."

22. I strongly value being orderly and tidy at work.

23. Companies should fire employees who give less than their full commitment to the job.

24. I often seem to have slow days at work.

25. I am known to be a very dependable person in keeping appointments.

26. Most people consider me very reliable if something needs to be done promptly.

*Reliability is a prime element in
conscientiousness. You certainly want to
affirm strongly agree with this statement.*

27. I can't stand people who change their social plans at the "last minute."

28. People who are often late to meetings can still be valuable employees.

29. I daydream a lot about what I would do if I won the lottery and could stop working.

30. People who can take early retirement from work are really lucky.

8

Extraversion: Are You the Life of the Party?

Among the first personality traits to be identified and measured is that of *extraversion* versus *introversion*. At the turn of the twentieth century, the innovative Swiss psychiatrist Carl Jung originated these terms to describe people who were either outer-directed or inner-directed in their emotional focus. During the ensuing decades, these terms have been influential in the way we perceive others.

Most people think of extraverts as "loud and talkative" and introverts as "quiet and withdrawn," but these descriptions have much wider significance. In essence, they are polar-opposite qualities that refer to persons' source of energy: what makes them feel alive and activated versus sluggish and depleted.

To provide a vivid example: Amidst a loud, boisterous party, some individuals quickly become giddy, excited, even exuberant, and find themselves charged up. But others, in the exact same party, soon feel sapped, drained, and even emotionally numb. Within the business world, extraversion has long been linked to effective salesmanship and regarded with favor. It's also been associated with the tendency to give off clear, easily readable facial expressions. Conversely, introverts have generally been criticized as bookish and self-absorbed, and offering little "readability" of facial expressions and moods.

It's important to understand that warmth and likability are separate from the extraversion/introversion dimension. There are plenty of extraverts who are cold and friendless—Michigan psychologist Dr. Russ Reeves aptly refers to them as "the car salesmen types with the dead eyes"—and there are many introverts with who are loving and enjoy deep friendships. The difference is that the extravert avoids aloneness and seeks out groups, whereas the introvert shuns crowds and seeks out relative solitude.

Of course, certain types of positions heavy on "number-crunching," like accounting, financial analysis, and computer programming, do not require you to be highly outgoing for successful performance. A moderate or even somewhat low score on extraversion is therefore unlikely to disqualify a candidate for such types of jobs. However, in an increasingly competitive global economy today, where so much work is organized in teams, an extraverted accountant, financial analyst, or computer programmer is more likely to be hired than his or her introverted counterpart.

Can you change your basic disposition from introversion to extraversion, or vice versa? Interestingly, psychological research indicates that this trait is among the most difficult of all to alter significantly. A vivid example is offered by President Richard Nixon.

A career politician with a relentless ambition for power, Nixon was by nature introverted; early in life, he was a highly diligent student—known as the "iron butt" at Duke Law School—and after leaving the presidency, he wrote several voluminous works on history and foreign relations. Nixon could never really alter this introverted tendency; but he could force himself to attend countless fund-raising parties, glad-hand at social gatherings, and engage in endless small talk—all in order to achieve his ambitious goals. Interestingly, his nemesis, Lyndon Johnson, was quite the opposite, and clearly showed strong extraversion. A more typical career politician than Nixon, President Johnson was highly charged by social functions (which he invariably tried to dominate) and assiduously avoided solitary activities like intellectual study and sustained writing.

Before tackling the sample personality tests that focus on extraversion, here are the three hiring zones that emanate from testing, and which, for job recruiters, significantly differentiate among candidates:

Definitely Hire:

This person is highly outgoing. She enjoys loud parties, finds it facile to meet new people, and is energized by the presence of others. Her emotional expressions can be easily "read," and she is adept at keeping a conversation flowing. In both work and leisure, she strongly prefers to interact with many different kinds of people rather than to engage in solitary activities.

Maybe Hire:

This person is relatively outgoing. She usually enjoys loud parties, finds it facile to meet new people, and is typically, but not always, energized by the presence of others. Generally, her emotional expressions can be easily "read," and she is able to keep a conversation flowing. On the whole, she prefers in both work and leisure to interact with different kinds of people rather than to engage in solitary activities.

Definitely Do Not Hire:

This person is not outgoing. She does not enjoy loud parties, finds it difficult to meet new people, and is usually drained by the presence of others. Her emotional expressions are hard to "read," and she is not skillful in keeping a conversation flowing. At both work and leisure, she prefers to engage in solitary activities rather than to interact with many different kinds of people.

Sample Test Questions

It's a sure thing that any personality test you take during the hiring process will include a scale designed to measure your extraversion. To help you master this scale, three sample tests—each comprising thirty questions that assess only the trait of extraversion—will follow. Be aware, though, that in the real-life situation, such questions will invariably be interspersed throughout the overall personality test you'll be taking and will definitely not appear consecutively or even grouped close together. Afterward, in the scoring procedure typically hidden from the candidate, his or her responses on this test are tabulated and an overall score is generated, together with its interpretation for the hiring entity.

EXTRAVERSION TEST #1

1. I am a good "mixer" in parties.

2. I am an easy person to get to know.

3. I am usually quiet and reserved in parties.

> *Many items regarding extraversion ask about your attitude toward parties, especially loud ones. Extraverts enjoy such affairs, and so would* strongly disagree *with this statement.*

4. Most people who know me describe me as a very open person.

5. In social settings I enjoy walking over and introducing myself to an unfamiliar person.

> *This item is crucial as a measure of extraversion. Of course, those who have this trait would* strongly agree *with the statement.*

6. I've been called a "social butterfly" by people who know me.

7. Being in a loud party excites me.

8. I almost never feel bored at parties.

> *Remember, extraverts love parties, so they would* strongly agree *with all such statements.*

9. It is easy for people to see my moods.

> *Another characteristic of extraverts is that their facial expressions are clear and "loud." So they would* strongly agree *with this statement.*

10. I easily make "small talk" when sitting next to a stranger on a plane or bus.

11. I enjoy chatting with strangers on a plane or bus.

12. I often have interesting conversations with people I meet for the first time.

13. Some of the most boring times I've had took place at loud parties.

14. I'm usually described as a very outgoing person.

> *Extraversion is often synonymous with being outgoing, so* strongly agree *is the appropriate response.*

15. I excel at keeping a conversation going.

> *An important trait of extraverts is their ability to converse well—so* strongly agree *is the fitting reply.*

16. In conversations, I like to let the other person do most of the talking.

> *Extraverts typically dominate conversations, so the appropriate response is* strongly disagree.

17. I rarely like to tell jokes to a group of people.

18. I like to be the center of attention at a party.

19. "The more the merrier" is my philosophy when it comes to socializing for the evening.

20. Most of my friends are quiet and reserved.

21. Nobody who knows me well would describe me as "the life of the party."

22. I must admit I am shy around large groups of people.

23. I get anxious when forced to meet strangers.

24. I like the feeling of being part of a large crowd at a parade.

25. Being part of a large crowd at a sporting event gives me a rush of energy.

26. I like to walk into a room full of unfamiliar people and start socializing.

27. I'd rather read a good book than socialize in a party.

28. I enjoy working alone.

29. If someone unfamiliar comes up to me in a party, I almost always feel comfortable about chatting.

30. I feel sorry for people who can't enjoy big parties.

EXTRAVERSION TEST #2

1. I am not a good "mixer" in parties.

2. I am not an easy person to get to know.

3. I am rarely quiet and reserved in parties.

4. Most people who know me would not describe me as a very open person.

5. In social settings, I avoid walking over and introducing myself to an unfamiliar person.

6. I've never been called a "social butterfly" by people who knew me.

7. Being in a loud party does not excite me.

8. I am often bored at parties.

9. It's difficult for people to know my moods.

10. It is hard for me to make "small talk" when sitting next to a stranger on a plane or bus.

11. I do not enjoy chatting with strangers on a plane or bus.

    Extraverts typically like to chat with strangers, so strongly disagree is the consistent answer.

12. I rarely have interesting conversations with new people I meet socially.

13. Some of the best times I've had took place at loud parties.

14. I'm seldom described as a very outgoing person.

15. I am not very good at keeping a conversation going.

16. In conversations, I rarely let the other person do most of the talking.

17. I often like to tell jokes to a group of people.

18. I avoid being the center of attention at a party.

    Extraverts can usually be found telling jokes and entertaining others—so strongly disagree would be the consistent reply.

19. "The more the merrier" is certainly not my philosophy when it comes to socializing for the evening.

    This old adage was surely coined by an extravert—thus, strongly disagree is the fitting reply.

20. Almost none of my friends are quiet and reserved.

    Usually, our friends resemble us personality-wise, so the fitting response is strongly agree for an extravert.

21. People who know me well would describe me as "the life of the party."

   This phrase describes in a nutshell the
   extravert; thus, strongly agree *is the*
   appropriate answer.

22. I never feel awkward in a large group of people.

23. I almost never feel tense when introducing myself to strangers.

24. I dislike being part of a big crowd at a parade.

25. Being part of a large crowd at a sporting event is very draining to me.

26. I dislike having to walk into a room full of unfamiliar people and start socializing.

27. I'd rather socialize in a party than read a book.

28. I dislike having to work alone.

29. If someone unfamiliar comes up to me in a party, I sometimes feel uncomfortable about chatting.

30. I feel empathy for people who don't enjoy big parties.

EXTRAVERSION TEST #3

1. I am a terrific "mixer" in parties.

2. I am a very easy person to get to know.

   Extraverts are typically open with their
   feelings and moods, so the correct response
   is strongly agree.

3. I am always quiet and reserved in parties.

4. Most people who know me regard me as a very open person.

5. In social settings, I enjoy strolling over and introducing myself to an unfamiliar person.

6. I've often been called a "social butterfly" by people who know me.

7. Being in a loud party is energizing for me.

8. I can't recall the last time I felt bored at a party.

9. I can find something to chat about with just about everyone.

10. I easily make "small talk" when sitting next to a stranger on a plane or bus.

11. I have become friends with people I first met as a stranger in a restaurant or café.

12. I often have fascinating conversations with strangers on a plane or bus.

13. Some of the most unpleasant times I've had took place at loud parties.

14. I'm generally regarded as a very outgoing person.

15. In conversations, I always let the other person do most of the talking.

16. I can't recall the last time I ever told a joke at a party.

17. I am usually the center of attention at a party.

18. "The more the merrier" is definitely my philosophy when it comes to socializing for the evening.

19. Most of my friends are on the shy side.

20. Nobody who really knows me would call me "the life of the party."

21. I must admit I get tongue-tied around new groups of people.

22. I sometimes avoid meeting new groups of people.

Extraverts would say the opposite, and thus strongly disagree with this statement.

23. It's exciting to me to be part of a large crowd at a parade.

24. Being part of a large crowd at a sporting event gives me a burst of energy.

Extraverts like such public gatherings, and so would strongly agree with this sentiment.

25. I'm skilled at walking into a room full of unfamiliar people and immediately begin socializing.

26. I'd rather listen to music alone than socialize in a party.

Extraverts would almost never prefer being alone to anything, except root-canal surgery. And so they would strongly disagree with all such statements.

27. I enjoy working by myself.

28. I find it more productive to work alone than to work as part of a group.

Extraverts dislike working alone just as much as spending leisure time alone. They would strongly disagree with this sentiment.

29. If someone unfamiliar comes up to me in a party, I almost always am glad afterward that they did.

30. There's something a bit odd about people who can't enjoy big parties.

9

Integrity: Are You Honest as the Day Is Long?

Testing for potentially dishonest employees has become a booming business today. Known as "integrity testing," it's a specialty that's currently in extremely high demand. Especially after the banning of lie detectors in the workplace, such personality measures have soared in managerial popularity. Virtually all measures are aimed at pinpointing as precisely as possible the job applicant who is likely to see his or her new position as a license to steal. Whether workers today are actually more likely to engage in thievery involving supplies, equipment, and paid time than in the past is a question for debate among human resource professionals. The consensus seems to be yes, worker honesty has diminished during the past generation—because organizational loyalty has largely disappeared in an era of massive layoffs, unprecedented downsizing, and reengineering at all levels. It's hardly a trend restricted to the United States; even in seemingly unchanging countries like Japan, where lifetime employment was almost guaranteed in exchange for unstinting loyalty to the enterprise, the equation is quickly altering.

Are you an honest person? To what extent? As I explained earlier in this book, job recruiters are not relying on personality tests as a means to uncover all-perfect human beings or saints, but rather, to weed out the potential troublemakers, hotheads, and misfits. And among these are folks who are likely to steal from their employers. Therefore, when it comes to honesty, only candidates who present themselves as scrupulously "squeaky clean" are likely to be hired.

Can a person overcome a tendency to steal in the workplace? Unfortunately, the psychological evidence is rather clear that antisocial behavior, including thievery, starts to manifest in childhood and often is full-blown by adolescence. Structured psychotherapy, particularly with a cognitive-behavioral emphasis (that is, on the individuals' thoughts and actions rather than on their childhood upbringing) can be effective, but definitely not for everybody.

In a world of habitual shoplifters and career criminals, many employers are rightfully worried about the damage their new hire can inflict. As a result, they would much rather have a few "false positives"—that is, honest candidates who get erroneously rejected as dishonest due to their responses—than allow a theft-minded candidate to join their organization.

Before tackling the sample personality tests that focus on *integrity*, here are the three hiring zones that emanate from testing, and which, for job recruiters, significantly differentiate among candidates:

Definitely Hire:

This person is honest and trustworthy. She has a strong sense of individual integrity. She sharply rejects permissive values regarding all forms of theft, including supplies, equipment, or company time. She clearly disassociates herself from coworkers who have less stringent attitudes about dishonest behavior.

Maybe Hire:

This person is essentially honest and trustworthy. She has a strong sense of individual integrity. She sharply rejects permissive values regarding most forms of theft, but expresses tolerance for seemingly minor infractions. She does not strongly disassociate herself from coworkers who have less stringent attitudes about dishonest behavior.

Definitely Do Not Hire:

This person is neither honest nor trustworthy. She lacks a strong sense of individual integrity. She embraces permissive values regarding many forms of theft, including supplies and company time. She does not disassociate herself from coworkers who are dishonest and lack integrity.

Sample Test Questions

It's certain that any personality test you take during the hiring process will include a scale aimed at measuring your integrity. To help you master this scale, three sample tests—each comprising thirty questions that assess only the trait of integrity—will follow. Be aware, though, that in the real-life situation, such questions will invariably be interspersed throughout the overall personality test you'll be taking and will definitely not appear consecutively or even grouped close together. Afterward, in the scoring procedure typically hidden from the candidate, his or her responses on this scale are tabulated and an overall score is generated, together with its interpretation for the hiring entity.

INTEGRITY TEST #1

1. Most people are honest by nature.

    *This is a crucial question. Managers must
    hear that you strongly agree with
    this statement if your candidacy
    is to be regarded favorably.*

2. If given the chance, most people would not steal a small item from a store if they knew they would never get caught.

3. Most people have never shoplifted as a child or teenager.

    *Managers want to hear that you regard
    shoplifting, at any age, as unusual and
    deviant. So the fitting reply is to strongly
    agree.*

4. Most people can be trusted.

    *Desirable candidates always strongly agree
    with this sentiment.*

5. Children who take money from a family member's purse or wallet should certainly be disciplined.

6. Parents should be very concerned about a child who steals from classmates.

7. Most youngsters do not steal from friends or classmates.

8. Few or none of the teenagers I knew in high school shoplifted at least once.

9. Parents should definitely make a fuss about a teenager who is caught shoplifting.

    *Those with high integrity strongly agree
    with this statement.*

10. High school teachers and principals should strongly discipline students who are caught shoplifting.

11. It's really not a primary duty of parents to teach their kids to be honest.

12. It can't be considered human nature to steal from others.

    *Those with high integrity strongly agree
    with this sentiment.*

13. I don't mind parents who think it's normal for kids to steal things.

14. I certainly believe someone who tells me that he/she never shoplifted as a teenager.

15. I believe that our society's laws against shoplifting are way too harsh.

    *Persons with high integrity strongly
    disagree with this view; if anything, they
    advocate harsher laws.*

16. If someone finds a wallet or purse in a store, it's wrong to take out any cash in it before handing it over to the manager.

17. Very few people in our society steal at work.

> *This is a tricky question. You don't want to suggest that you consider stealing to be normal due to its commonness. Thus, to agree is probably the most fitting reply.*

18. Employees who leave work early without permission are not really stealing from their company.

19. It's wrong to call in sick occasionally to take a day off for rest and relaxation.

20. Employees who call in sick frequently probably just need the rest.

21. An employee who sees a coworker taking supplies home should not report it to the supervisor.

22. An employee who occasionally takes supplies home is not really stealing.

23. Not all employees take home supplies now and then from work.

24. An employee who is caught taking minor supplies home even once should definitely not be fired.

25. If someone is undercharged in a restaurant, he/she should not tell the waiter/waitress.

26. It is wrong to buy merchandise that you know is stolen.

27. If an employee accidentally receives too much money in a paycheck, it is a form of stealing not to report it.

28. A company should sometimes hire a person who was fired from his/her last job for stealing.

29. If I found a bag of money on the street, I would seriously think about keeping it.

30. Most of my friends are extremely honest.

INTEGRITY TEST #2

1. Most people are dishonest by nature.

2. If allowed the opportunity, most people would steal a small item from a store if they knew they would never get caught.

> *People with high integrity certainly strongly disagree with this statement.*

3. Nearly everybody has shoplifted as a child or teenager.

4. Most people cannot be trusted.

5. A child who takes money from a classmate is just doing something natural.

6. Parents should not get overly worried about a child who steals from class-mates.

7. It's perfectly natural for a teenager to shoplift.

8. Nearly all my friends stole something as children at least once.

9. Parents should never make a fuss about a teenager who is caught shoplift-ing.

10. High school teachers and principals often get too upset about students who are caught shoplifting.

11. Some of my friends are not very honest.

12. I am outraged by parents who fail to teach their kids to be honest.

   High integrity persons can certainly feel
   outraged by such poor child-rearing, so
   to strongly agree *is fitting.*

13. It's simply human nature to steal a little.

14. It's not foolish for parents to expect that a youngster will never steal from a classmate.

   Those with high integrity maintain very high
   standards for ethical behavior, and so
   would strongly agree *with this statement.*

15. I don't believe someone who tells me that he/she never shoplifted as a teenager.

16. I believe that our society's laws against shoplifting should be made much tougher.

17. People who keep the money they find in a wallet or purse on the street are not really stealing.

18. Far too many people in our society steal at work.

19. Employees who leave work early without permission are stealing from their company.

   Managers want to hear that a candidate
   strongly agrees *with such a sentiment.*

20. It's perfectly okay to call in sick occasionally to take a day off for rest and relax-ation.

   High integrity employees never engage in
   sick-ins, and thus would strongly
   disagree *with this statement.*

21. Employees who call in sick too often should be fired.

22. An employee who sees a coworker taking supplies home should immediately report it to the supervisor.

23. An employee who is caught taking minor supplies home even once should be fired.

24. There should be zero tolerance at work for employees who take home supplies, even minor items.

25. If someone is undercharged in a supermarket, he/she should tell the cashier.

26. It is okay to buy merchandise occasionally that you know is stolen.

27. If an employee accidentally receives too much money in a paycheck, it's just common sense not to report it.

28. A company should not hire a person who was fired from his/her last job for stealing.

29. If I found a bag of money on the street, I would not seriously think about keeping it.

30. I don't think anyone is totally honest.

INTEGRITY TEST #3

1. People are basically honest by nature.

2. If given the chance, most people would steal a small item from a store if they knew they would never get caught.

3. Few people ever shoplifted as a child or teenager.

4. Generally, people can be trusted.

5. Children who take money from a family member's purse or wallet should definitely face consequences.

6. A child who takes money from a classmate should definitely be disciplined.

7. Parents should definitely be concerned about a child who steals from classmates.

8. Few youngsters steal from friends or classmates.

9. It's not typical for a teenager to shoplift.

10. Nobody in my crowd in high school ever shoplifted.

11. Parents should be concerned about a teenager who is caught shoplifting.

12. High school teachers and principals should deal strongly with students who are caught shoplifting.

13. I am not very disturbed about parents who fail to teach their kids to be honest.

14. I detest parents who think it's normal for kids to steal things.

15. I can well believe someone who tells me he/she never shoplifted as a teenager.

16. I believe that our society's laws against shoplifting are too harsh.

17. If someone finds a wallet or purse in a store, it's like stealing to take out the cash before handing it over to the manager.

18. It's not common for people in our society to steal at work.

19. Employees who leave work early without permission should not be considered as stealing from their company.

20. An employee is wrong to call in sick occasionally to take a day off for rest and relaxation.

21. Employees who call in sick often probably just need the rest.

22. Companies are not unreasonable if they expect their employees to never call in sick when they need a day off.

23. An employee who sees a coworker taking supplies home should not be expected to tell the supervisor.

24. Employees who sometimes take supplies home are not really stealing.

> *Only those lacking in integrity would fail to*
>   *strongly disagree with this statement.*

25. If someone is undercharged in a convenience store, he/she should tell the cashier.

> *The high integrity person would not hesitate*
>   *to strongly agree with this viewpoint.*

26. It is definitely not right to buy merchandise that you know is stolen.

27. If an employee accidentally receives too much money in a paycheck, it is like stealing not to report it.

> *Managers certainly expect that employees*
>   *with adequate integrity would strongly*
>   *agree with this statement.*

28. A company should be willing to hire a person who was fired from his/her last job for stealing.

29. If I found a bag of money on the street, I would probably think about keeping it.

30. All of my friends are honest.

10

Going Postal: Are You Feeling Angry?

Unless you've arrived from another planet lately, you know that workplace rage is a major concern in today's organizational world. Such phrases as "going postal" (describing an employee on the rampage), "road rage," and "air rage" have all have become new additions to the English language.

In the action-thriller film, *The Rock,* FBI agent Stanley Goodspeed, played by actor Nicholas Cage, exclaims, "There's a lot of anger expressed here, I can just *feel* it!" He makes this point after being seized on Alcatraz Island by a band of vengeful American terrorists intent on mayhem, but he just as easily could have been referring to today's workplace, for research clearly shows greater rage among employees than ever before.

Indeed, workplace violence was recently rated the main threat to America's largest corporations, according to a survey of Fortune 1000 security executives. The Workplace Violence Research Institute based in Palm Springs, California, has estimated that on-the-job violence specifically costs employers at least $36 billion annually, up *850 percent* over the last five years. And the U.S. Department of Justice estimates that those victimized at the workplace comprise 500,000 employees and lose an average of 3.5 days of work per crime.

As a result, companies are putting a lot of effort into screening out potentially enraged, violent employees. Under the legal doctrine of "negligent hiring," firms' recruiters are potentially liable for the harmful actions committed by those they've brought on board. By failing to administer appropriate personality tests to assess for those who are violence prone—or so the current legal argument goes—such enterprises are guilty of negligence, just as they would be for allowing incompetent contractors to install a defective elevator system that later malfunctions and injures employees.

Can you really alter an angry personality through counseling or therapy? The experts themselves aren't sure, though a client's actual motivation for change is paramount. For instance, it's known that the teenage killers of Columbine High School successfully completed an "anger management" course as a consequence for their earlier antisocial behavior. Yet, at the same time they were participating in this course, the two were actively plotting their school's horrific destruction.

Before tackling the sample personality tests that focus on rage readiness, here are the three hiring zones that emanate from testing, and which, for job recruiters, decisively differentiate among candidates:

Definitely Hire:

This person does not have anger or resentment. He believes that anger is never justifiable and strongly disapproves of anger-generated behavior as a means to deal with problems in many different settings. He poses no discernible risk for committing violence in the workplace.

Maybe Hire:

This person does not have a significant amount of anger or resentment. He believes that anger is only rarely justifiable and generally disapproves of anger-generated behavior as a means to deal with problems in many different settings. He poses low risk for committing violence in the workplace.

Definitely Do Not Hire:

This person is a walking time-bomb. He is filled with rage and lacks the ability to cope with it effectively. He believes that his anger is justifiable and approves of anger-generated behavior as a means to deal with problems in diverse settings. He poses a high risk for committing violence in the workplace.

Sample Test Questions

It's a sure thing that any personality test you take during the hiring process will include a scale designed to measure your anger. To help you master this scale, three sample tests—each comprising thirty questions that assess only the trait of anger—will follow. Be aware, though, that in the real-life situation such questions will invariably be interspersed throughout the overall personality test you'll be taking and will definitely not appear consecutively or even grouped close together. Afterward, in the scoring procedure typically hidden from the candidate, his or her responses on this test are tabulated and an overall score is generated, together with its interpretation for the hiring entity.

"GOING POSTAL" TEST #1

1. I have sometimes gotten angry at work.

    *Managers know you're no saint, but they
    don't want to hear that you ever get angry*

on the job. To strongly disagree *is the fitting reply.*

2. I've had a lot of irritating coworkers lately.

   Managers also know that some employees are irritating, but they don't want to hear that you've been encountering them. Therefore, to strongly disagree *is appropriate.*

3. In my opinion, most employees have fantasized about harming their supervisors.

4. I don't believe in getting angry. I believe in getting even.

   You can be sure that a candidate who fails to strongly disagree *with this statement will not be regarded favorably for hiring.*

5. It's normal to lose your temper at work from time to time.

   Whether this statement is psychologically true or not, the desirable candidate will strongly disagree *with it.*

6. Sometimes in my car I get really angry at the stupidities of other drivers.

   Road rage may be common, but the desirable candidate strongly disagrees *with this statement.*

7. In some cases when a student hits a teacher, that teacher actually deserves it.

8. I get mad if a supermarket clerk keeps me waiting too long in line.

   The desirable candidate is always calm and strongly disagrees *with such statements.*

9. It must be admitted that almost everyone fantasizes about destroying equipment at work.

   No, they don't. And if you fail to strongly disagree, *your likelihood of being hired is minimal.*

10. Employees who destroy equipment at work sometimes have a good reason for doing so.

11. Nearly all high school students have fantasized about getting even with a teacher.

12. If I saw a coworker jokingly write a threatening e-mail before erasing it, I would tell my supervisor.

13. Computer hackers are sometimes punished too severely for just having some fun.

14. People who know me well say I have a temper.

15. It wouldn't be true to say I never get angry at work.

16. Sometimes, I've felt so angry at work that I had to step outside for a "breather."

17. I don't believe people who say they never lose their temper at work.

18. I think almost everybody carries around at least some anger toward a coworker or supervisor.

19. People who get angry on the job have a big problem that may need to be treated by counseling.

20. Sometimes, no matter how hard people try, they can't control their anger, and therefore shouldn't be blamed for it.

21. I would report a coworker who I saw angrily kicking a bathroom door.

22. I would report a coworker who I overheard in the bathroom muttering threats about "getting back" at the supervisor.

23. I have sometimes angrily insulted a coworker, but then immediately apologized.

24. At times at home, I have lost my temper in a big way.

25. People who cannot always control their anger should be fired.

26. All this talk about "road rage" is exaggerated.

27. I have sometimes been afraid of my own temper.

28. People who know me would never describe me as hot-tempered or hot-headed.

29. If someone starts to insult me, he or she had better watch out.

30. I have sometimes gotten mad after being put "on hold" for a long time on the phone.

"GOING POSTAL" TEST #2

1. I have never lost my temper at work.

2. I've had no irritating coworkers lately.

3. In my opinion, most employees have not fantasized about harming their supervisors.

4. I would not hire someone who said, "I don't believe in getting angry. I believe in getting even."

5. It's not normal to lose your temper at work from time to time.

6. I never get really angry at the stupidities of other drivers.

7. It's never justifiable for a student to hit an insulting teacher.

   *Employees who are low on anger would
   certainly* strongly agree *with this
   sentiment.*

8. An employee who sends a threatening e-mail to a coworker should be fired immediately.

9. It's not true that almost everyone fantasizes about destroying equipment at work.

10. If someone cuts in front of me in line at the post office, I don't really mind.

11. Most high school students have not fantasized about getting even with a teacher.

12. It's not true that the only way a supervisor gets the point is when an employee secretly destroys some equipment.

13. Computer hackers are sometimes punished too lightly.

    *Workplace sabotage is a growing problem, and
    not taken lightly by managers at all. To
    strongly agree is the appropriate answer.*

14. People who know me well would not say I have a temper.

    *The desirable candidate has no anger problem,
    period, and would thus strongly agree
    with this statement.*

15. It wouldn't be true to say I often get angry at work.

16. I've never felt so angry at work that I had to step outside for a "breather."

17. I believe people who say they never lose their temper at work.

18. I don't think that most employees carry around at least some anger toward a coworker or supervisor.

19. People who get angry on the job have a big problem that should be treated by immediate counseling.

    *People low on anger would strongly agree
    with this viewpoint.*

20. Sometimes, no matter how hard people try, they can't control their anger, but they are responsible for their actions.

21. I would not report a coworker who I saw angrily kicking a bathroom door.

    *There's probably so much apprehension today
    about workplace rage that the fitting reply
    would be to strongly agree with all such
    statements about witnessed explosiveness.*

22. I would not report a coworker who I overheard in the bathroom muttering threats about "getting back" at the supervisor.

23. I can't recall ever having angrily insulted a coworker.

24. At home, I have never lost my temper in a big way.

25. People who cannot always control their anger should consider taking medication.

26. It's sometimes understandable why employees lose their temper at work.

27. I have never been afraid of my own temper.

28. People who know me would describe me as occasionally hot-tempered or hotheaded.

29. I never lose my temper after getting poor service at a restaurant.

30. I have never gotten into an argument with a clerk in a retail store.

"GOING POSTAL" TEST #3

1. I have never felt enraged at work.

2. I've had very few irritating coworkers in my career.

3. In my view, the majority of employees have never fantasized about harming their supervisors.

4. I would never hire someone who said, "I don't believe in getting angry. I believe in getting even."

   Those with low anger have zero tolerance for such vengeful types, and would therefore strongly agree *with such statements.*

5. It's not normal to lose your temper at work even occasionally.

6. I sometimes get angry at the stupidities of other drivers.

7. It's sometimes justifiable for a student to hit an insulting classmate.

8. I never get mad if a postal clerk keeps me waiting too long in line.

9. I don't believe that almost all employees fantasize about destroying equipment at work.

10. Employees who destroy equipment at work occasionally have a good reason for doing so.

11. Very few high school students have fantasized about getting even with a teacher.

12. I don't believe that sometimes the only way a supervisor gets the point is when an employee secretly destroys some equipment.

13. Computer hackers are usually punished too lightly.

14. People who know me well would admit I have a temper.

15. It would be false to say I often get angry at work.

16. I can't imagine ever feeling so angry at work that I had to step outside for a "breather."

Only those high in anger would fail to strongly agree with this statement.

17. I have many friends who have never lost their temper at work.

18. I don't think that the majority of employees carry around at least some anger toward a coworker or supervisor.

19. People who get angry on the job have a big problem, and it is therefore justifiable to fire them.

20. Sometimes, no matter how hard people try, they can't control their anger, but they are always responsible for their actions.

21. I would probably report a coworker who I saw angrily kicking a bathroom door.

22. I would probably report a coworker who I overheard in the bathroom muttering threats about "getting back" at the supervisor.

23. I can't recall ever having angrily insulted anyone at work.

24. At home, I have never lost my temper at a family member.

25. People who cannot always control their anger may need to take medication.

26. In a lot of companies, it's very understandable why employees lose their temper at work.

27. I am often afraid of my own temper.

28. People who know me would describe me as soft-spoken and soft-tempered.

29. I can't remember getting into an argument with a clerk at a retail store.

Arguing isn't rage, but managers are wary of hiring those who fly off the handle easily. Therefore, to strongly agree is the fitting reply.

30. I have sometimes lost my temper after getting poor service at a restaurant.

11
Are You Entrepreneurial?

In this high-tech era, everyone wants to run their own business, right? Everybody wants to establish and create their own company, isn't that so? Not only are such views incorrect, but perhaps even more important, many would-be entrepreneurs lack the crucial psychological traits for generating their own organization—however small or large it may ultimately become. Maybe a larger number of people suspect this truth than they let on, for otherwise, we would probably see many more businesses created than actually exist.

Certainly, entrepreneurship has gained increasing popularity with the phenomenal growth of the Internet and the riches that many "dotcom" companies seemed to have produced for their invested staff and outside shareholders. Yet, for more than a generation, organizational thinkers have recognized that business achievement is not synonymous with entrepreneurial ability. For example, those who successfully lead Fortune 500 companies are not necessarily equally adept in starting new enterprises. Rather, a different and highly specific set of personality qualities seems to be involved; so much so, in fact, that business psychology studies have shown that it's possible to predict the long-term viability of start-up enterprises by knowing the entrepreneurial test score of their founders/leaders.

If not everybody is cut out to start a business from scratch, can the necessary personality traits be learned? After all, aren't there schools—even highly respected university programs nowadays—devoted to entrepreneurship? Doesn't the existence of such schools indicate that people can absorb the necessary attributes of successful entrepreneurs?

The answer is a qualified no. Through competent training, individuals can certainly improve their savvy and skills in matters of finance, marketing, and sales, which intertwine with all types of firms, including start-ups. In this sense, schools of entrepreneurship have a definite role to offer would-be business founders. But psychological research has clearly revealed that entrepreneurs possess certain specific personality traits—above all, the ability to take risks and to trust intuition—that cannot really be "taught" the way one teaches elementary accounting or brand-name marketing. Indeed, there is even growing evidence that the entrepreneurial personality may be genetically influenced or determined—and hence even less likely to be "learned" than theorists previously believed.

Before tackling the sample personality tests that focus on entrepreneurialism, here are the three hiring zones that emanate from testing, and which, for job recruiters, meaningfully differentiate among candidates:

Definitely Hire:

This person takes risks and values risk-taking as an important aspect of success. She relies strongly on her intuitions and is willing to make decisions when there is not a plethora of information. She has an optimistic view of life and of personal achievement.

Maybe Hire:

This person is sometimes willing to take risks and has a positive attitude toward risk-taking. She often follows her intuitions and is sometimes willing to make decisions in the absence of clear information. She has a fairly optimistic view of life and of personal achievement.

Definitely Do Not Hire:

This person avoids risks and criticizes risk-taking as an important determinant of success. She shuns her intuitions and is unwilling to make decisions when there is not a great deal of information. She has a pessimistic view of life and of personal achievement.

Sample Test Questions

With both start-up companies and well-established firms creating divisions emulating these, it's likely that your personality evaluation will include a scale aimed at measuring your entrepreneurialism. To help you master this scale, three sample tests—each containing thirty questions that assess only the trait of entrepreneurialism—will follow. Be aware, though, that in the real-life situation such questions will invariably be interspersed throughout the overall personality test you'll be taking and will definitely not appear consecutively or even grouped close together. Afterward, in the scoring procedure typically hidden from the candidate, his or her responses on this scale are tabulated and an overall score is generated, together with its interpretation for the hiring entity.

TEST OF ENTREPRENEURIALISM #1

1. Life is full of risks.

2. You can't really be successful in life if you're afraid of failure.

   An ability to take risks and minimize the permanency of failure are vital to entrepreneurship. Strongly agree is therefore consistent.

3. I like to make decisions when there's not a lot of information available.

4. I am optimistic about the future.

5. I don't get bored easily.

6. I like to try new foods and sensations.

   Many personality tests use items similar to this one. To strongly agree is associated with the entrepreneurial personality.

7. People who know me well would describe me as a risk-taker.

8. In my opinion, listening to one's "hunches" is important in achieving success.

9. A lot of errors in business are caused by taking foolish chances.

10. I believe that people who are afraid to take risks did not have effective parents.

11. It's foolish to make a decision unless you have a lot of solid information to guide you.

    Another key trait of entrepreneurs is their willingness to trust personal hunches. Strongly disagree is thus consistent.

12. I certainly believe that people can be too cautious in business or work.

13. Without new projects to keep me interested, work would be unsatisfying to me.

    Even in big companies nowadays, entrepreneurial types are being wooed and promoted. Such persons seek new projects frequently, so strongly agree is consistent.

14. Many people take too many chances in business and work for their own good.

15. Parents should encourage their kids to be cautious in making decisions.

16. When all is said and done, it's the risk-takers who have the most success in life.

17. I like to do something new every day.

18. People who get bored easily have something wrong with them.

19. I agree with the old Chinese saying, "The first bird flying out of the forest is the one who gets shot by the hunters—because he leaves the flock."

20. People would never think me of as a pioneer or trailblazer at work.

> *To strongly disagree supports your contention that you're entrepreneurial in nature.*

21. I greatly admire the early pioneers who settled the United States.

22. Compared to most people I know, I am definitely a risk-taker.

> *Strongly agree is the answer linked to the entrepreneur.*

23. Schools should teach kids more about how to make decisions by acting on their "gut" or intuition.

24. I believe that coming up with new ideas and methods is a sure way to success.

25. The thought of starting a new business is appealing to me.

26. The future excites me.

> *Unless one is forward-thinking, entrepreneurialism makes no sense. Strongly agree is the consistent response.*

27. Compared to most people my age, I have been rather cautious in career and work pursuits.

28. "Take a chance" is my philosophy of life.

29. I like to seek out new restaurants.

30. "Be deliberate in all that you do" is not a very useful approach to success.

TEST OF ENTREPRENEURIALISM #2

1. It's nonsense to say that life is full of risks.

2. You can be most successful in life if you avoid taking risks.

3. I hate to make a decision when there isn't a lot of information available.

> *A feature of the entrepreneurial personality is the readiness to make decisions without "all the facts" available. So strongly disagree is appropriate.*

4. I am gloomy about the future.

5. I get bored very easily.

> *The entrepreneur is never bored. Strongly*
> disagree *is the only sensible reply.*

6. I do not like to try new foods and sensations.

7. People who know me well would not describe me as a risk-taker.

> *The entrepreneur's friends and associates*
> *know his or her personality and would*
> strongly disagree *with this statement.*

8. In my opinion, listening to one's "hunches" often leads to bad results.

9. A lot of failure in business or work is due to acting too cautiously.

10. I believe that people who avoid taking risks are, in a way, to be admired.

11. It's never foolish to make a decision without a lot of solid information to guide you.

12. It's nonsense to think that people can be too cautious in business or work.

13. Without new projects to keep me interested, work would not be unsatisfying to me.

14. Many people take too few risks in business and work for their own good.

15. Parents should not encourage their kids to be cautious in making decisions.

> *Most entrepreneurs say they were*
> *encouraged by their parents to act*
> *decisively, and consequently would*
> strongly agree *with this statement.*

16. When all is said and done, it's the risk-takers who are often least successful in life.

17. I do not want to do something new every day.

18. People who get bored easily are usually creative types.

> *Virtually all entrepreneurs would* strongly
> agree *with this statement.*

19. I disagree with the old Chinese saying, "The first bird flying out of the forest is the one who gets shot by the hunter—because he leaves the flock."

20. People sometimes view me of as a pioneer or trailblazer at work.

21. I sometimes look at the early pioneers who settled the United States as foolhardy.

22. Compared to most people I know, I am definitely not a risk-taker.

23. Schools should teach kids more about how to make decisions using only solid information.

24. I believe that coming up with new ideas and methods is no guarantee of success.

25. The thought of starting a new business is not appealing to me.

26. The future really makes me excited.

27. Compared to most people my age, I have not been cautious in career and work pursuits.

28. "Take a chance" could not be described as my philosophy of life.

29. "Be deliberate in all that you do" is a useful approach to success.

TEST OF ENTREPRENEURIALISM #3

1. We cannot avoid taking risks in life.

2. You can't really be a high-achiever if you don't take risks.

3. I enjoy making decisions when there isn't a lot of information available.

4. I am very optimistic about the future.

5. I never get bored by doing familiar things and routines.

6. I like to sample new foods and sensations.

7. People who know me well would refer to me as a risk-taker.

8. In my opinion, listening to one's "hunches" is important in becoming successful.

9. A lot of failure in business or work is due to acting on "gut" or "instinct."

10. I believe that people who habitually avoid taking risks had ineffective parents.

11. It's silly to make a decision until you have a lot of solid information available.

12. I believe that people can miss out on opportunities by being too cautious in business or work.

    Entrepreneurs would certainly strongly agree with this statement.

13. Without new things to keep me interested, work would be very unsatisfying to me.

14. In general, people take too many risks in business and work for their own good.

15. Parents should encourage their kids to be prudent in making decisions.

16. When all is said and done, it's the risk-takers who gain fame and fortune in life.

17. I enjoy doing something new every day.

18. People who get bored easily have a flaw.

19. I support the old Chinese saying, "The first bird flying out of the forest is the one who gets shot by the hunter—because he leaves the flock."

    Entrepreneurs would strongly disagree *with this cautionary statement.*

20. People would rarely think of me of as a pioneer or trailblazer at work.

21. I admire people who try to invent new products and services.

22. Compared to most people I know, I could be considered a risk-taker.

23. Schools should teach kids more about how to make decisions by acting on their "hunches."

24. I believe that being prudent is a trait of successful people.

25. The thought of developing a new business excites me.

    Of course, it's basic for entrepreneurs to enjoy the challenge of starting a new business; they would strongly agree *with this statement.*

26. The future seems wonderful to me.

27. Compared to most people my age, I have been cautious in career and work pursuits.

28. "Take a chance" is my attitude toward life.

29. I like to seek out new parks and places to visit.

30. "Be deliberate in all that you do" is not something I would usually advise.

12
Stress Tolerance: Can You Keep Your Cool?

In the new "Information Age" economy—both in the United States and abroad—stress has become ever more pervasive on the job. Employees are indeed working longer hours than ever before, and in an increasingly competitive global marketplace, the "slack" that was once common—remember the era of leisurely lunches at relaxing restaurants?—has almost completely disappeared. If you're nostalgic, get with it. A return to the pre-Internet pace of doing business is as likely as the triumphant reemergence of typewriters, carbon paper, slide rules, or black-and-white television. We're all getting more and more wired, even elementary school kids with their beepers, screen names, and e-mail accounts.

So, psychologically speaking, nearly everyone is facing more stress at work these days. Company presidents, executive managers, and senior administrators certainly know this to be true, for they're experiencing it themselves. The question for recruiters, therefore, isn't whether you'll have to deal with occasional on-the-job stress, but how emotionally stable and strong are you to cope with it regularly. It's highly expected nowadays—virtually guaranteed—that you'll be encountering potentially stressful situations almost daily involving deadlines, long hours, high-pressure meetings, and that you'll have few opportunities to really unwind. To be sure, some enterprises are providing on-site stress-reduction facilities like gyms, swimming pools, aerobic and yoga classes, and even aromatherapy and licensed masseurs, but don't expect employee stress to fade totally into the background.

Can you learn to cope with stress more effectively if that's not your forte? Absolutely. Over the past decade, a substantial body of medical and psychological research has emerged to show that nearly everyone can learn to handle job tensions more effectively, though we differ in what particular activities are most pleasurable. One point to keep in mind: People benefit more from structured stress-management programs, such as those associated with a health club or employee assistance program, rather than from "winging" it individually and without supervision.

Before tackling the sample personality tests that focus on proneness to stress, here are the three hiring zones that emanate from testing, and which, for job recruiters, meaningfully differentiate among candidates:

Definitely Hire:

This person deals with stress well. He maintains a calm disposition and his reactions are all acceptable. He does not suffer any health consequences from stress. Tension at work is something he takes in stride, and it does not interfere with his emotional or physical stability in any significant way. This person's proneness to stress has a minimal impact on his productivity.

Maybe Hire:

This person is semisuccessful in meeting stress at work. He usually maintains a calm demeanor and his reactions are generally, but not always, acceptable. Tension at work is something that sometimes throws him off stride. At times it impacts significantly on his emotional or physical stability. This person's proneness to stress has a moderate impact on his productivity.

Definitely Do Not Hire:

This person is a failure in responding to stress at work. He is unable to maintain a calm demeanor, and his reactions are often unacceptable. Tension at work is something that he has never mastered adequately, and it frequently impacts adversely on his emotional or physical stability. This person's proneness to stress has a severe effect on his productivity.

Sample Test Questions

It's a sure thing that any personality test you take during the hiring process will include a scale designed to measure your ability to cope with stress. To help you master this scale, three sample tests—each comprising thirty questions that assess only the trait of stress tolerance—will follow. Be aware, though, that in the real-life situation, such questions will invariably be interspersed throughout the overall personality test you'll be taking and will definitely not appear consecutively or even grouped close together. Afterward, in the scoring procedure typically hidden from the candidate, his or her responses on this scale are tabulated and an overall score is generated, together with its interpretation for the hiring entity.

STRESS TOLERANCE TEST #1

1. I have sometimes felt very stressed at work.

2. I would like to learn how to handle work stress better.

    *This question is a little tricky. You don't want
    to admit to being overwhelmed by stress,
    but you do want to show your eagerness to
    improve on the job.* Neutral *is probably
    the fitting reply.*

3. I have never found it hard to unwind after work.

4. I have sometimes lost sleep worrying about work.

5. I never worry about how well I am doing at my job.

    *This question is also a little tricky. Note the
    word* never. *It is probably more
    appropriate to* agree *with this statement.*

6. I feel anxious when I think about my work in the future.

7. Sometimes I don't feel able to handle all my work responsibilities.

    *One of the worst signs of poor stress-tolerance
    is to lose self-confidence. To* strongly
    disagree *is therefore the fitting answer.*

8. I have sometimes felt so worried about my job competence that I've had stomach problems.

9. I have sometimes snapped at a coworker because of tension.

    *To lose social skills due to stress is a bad sign.
    The successful candidate would* strongly
    disagree *with this statement.*

10. I don't know how some people can get through their workday without feeling stress.

11. Work is the most stressful thing in my life.

    *Whatever gives you stress in your life,
    managers don't want to hear that it
    involves work. Therefore, to* strongly
    disagree *is the fitting reply.*

12. I never get upset if my work is criticized by my boss.

    *Being able to handle criticism well is a sign of
    emotional maturity and calmness, so to
    strongly* agree *is the consistent answer.*

13. I have sometimes felt so much stress at work that I actually became sick.

*Managers certainly don't want to hear that
you may exhibit absenteeism due to stress.
To strongly disagree is the appropriate
sentiment.*

14. I worry that I am working too hard.
15. I have never worried about losing my job because of office politics.
16. I seem to get into constant arguments at work.
17. I have sometimes felt exhausted at the end of my workday.
18. I have sometimes had an anxiety dream about work.
19. I often daydream about relaxing vacations.
20. I know a lot of people who seem to be able to handle work stress better than I do.
21. I have sometimes cried after work because of an argument or problem I had there.
22. I have often felt like quitting a job because of work stress.
23. I often find myself thinking about work even when I try to relax.
24. I sometimes eat too much because of work tensions.
25. I have never drunk too much alcohol because of work stress.
26. I find it hard to laugh sometimes because of tensions spilling over from work.
27. I have suffered weight loss or weight gain due to work stress.
28. I have never lost my temper with a family member because of stress from work.
29. I have sometimes felt so much stress at work that I needed counseling.
30. If I could handle work stress better, I would be a lot more successful.

STRESS TOLERANCE TEST #2

1. I frequently feel stressed at work.
2. I would like to cope better with work stress.
3. I often find it hard to unwind after work.
4. I have never lost sleep worrying about work.
5. I often worry about how well I am doing at my job.
6. I feel confident when I think about my work in the future.
7. I am optimistic about my ability to cope with changes on the job.

> *Optimism has been found to be an important*
> *sign of mental health, on the job and off. To*
> *strongly agree is the fitting reply.*

8. I have never felt so worried about my job competence that I had stomach problems.

9. I drink too much coffee at work.

> *Managers don't care if you consume lots of*
> *coffee; many do, too. To disagree is*
> *certainly an acceptable answer.*

10. Work has never been the most stressful thing in my life.

11. I often get upset if my work is criticized by my boss.

12. I have never felt so much stress at work that I actually became sick.

13. I never worry whether I am working too hard.

14. I have sometimes worried about losing my job because of office politics.

> *You definitely don't want to give the*
> *impression that you have trouble with*
> *office politics. To strongly disagree is the*
> *relevant reply.*

15. I handle myself well with coworkers.

> *Good social skills are deemed crucial for most*
> *jobs today—so strongly agree is the*
> *appropriate answer.*

16. I rarely feel drained at the end of my workday.

17. I can't recall ever having had an anxiety dream about work.

18. I rarely fantasize about taking a relaxing vacation.

19. I don't know anyone who seems better able to handle work stress than I do.

20. I have sometimes cried on the job because of a work-related argument or problem.

21. I have never started job hunting because of work stress.

22. I am always able to relax after the workday.

23. I can't recall ever having eaten too much because of work tensions.

24. I have sometimes smoked too many cigarettes because of work stress.

25. I have sometimes suffered weight loss or gain due to work tensions.

26. I have sometimes lost my temper with a family member because of stress from work.

27. I have never had so much stress at work that I needed counseling.

Unfortunately, to admit to counseling or
therapy can cost a candidate his or her
hoped-for job. To strongly disagree *is the*
reply that managers want to hear.

28. I am proud of my ability to handle work without ever becoming tense.

29. I often feel I am performing inadequately at work.

30. I never worry about my job performance.

STRESS TOLERANCE TEST #3

1. Hardly a day goes by at work without my feeling stressed.

2. I have learned to handle work stress very well.

3. It's easy for me to unwind after work.

4. I have sometimes tossed in my sleep worrying about work.

   Managers don't want to hear that you've had
   sleep problems, which can lead to
   absenteeism. So to strongly disagree *is*
   the appropriate reply.

5. I can't recall the last time that I worried how well I was doing at my job.

6. I feel tense in thinking about my work in the future.

7. I have a lot of confidence in my ability to handle my work responsibilities.

   A sign of emotional well-being is self-
   confidence. So to strongly agree *is*
   the fitting reply.

8. I felt so worried about my job competence that I had stomach problems.

9. I have never snapped at a coworker because I felt tense.

10. I think stress is basic to almost all jobs nowadays.

11. I would have to admit that work is the most stressful thing in my life.

12. I rarely get upset if my work is criticized by my boss.

13. I have sometimes felt so much stress at work that I called in sick the next day.

    Unless you're an extremely desired candidate,
    to answer anything but strongly disagree
    with this statement can cost you the
    hoped-for job.

14. I worry that I sometimes work so hard that my health suffers.

15. I have often worried about losing my job because of office politics.

16. I get into silly arguments a lot at work.

17. I have sometimes felt ready to fall asleep at the end of my workday.

18. I have frequently had anxiety dreams about work.

19. I'd love to take a long, relaxing vacation.

20. Some of my friends seem to be able to handle work stress better than I do.

21. I have never cried after work because of an argument or problem I had there.

22. I have quit a job because of work stress.

23. Sometimes I find myself thinking about work even when I try to relax.

24. I often eat too much because of work tensions.

25. I often drink too much alcohol because of work stress.

26. I find it hard to enjoy my leisure sometimes because of my worries about work.

27. I have often suffered weight loss or weight gain due to work stress.

28. I can't recall ever losing my temper with a family member because of stress from work.

29. I have sometimes felt so much stress at work that I thought about getting counseling.

30. I rarely feel that I am performing inadequately at work.

13

Leadership: Do You Have the Right Stuff?

"Leaders are born, not made" is a classic aphorism. Reflecting the influence of powerful figures like Napoleon Bonaparte, who arose out of obscurity and poverty to shake the world, is it an observation still true? Certainly, the many books being published today on organizational leadership suggest that the tide of opinion has altered. In an era of tremendous global economic change, large enterprises especially are interested in long-range planning to stay competitive, successful, and growthful, and they're eager to recruit individuals who can steer a course with vision and fortitude.

Can you fit the bill? Most of the psychological studies on leadership capacity stress three elements:

1. Optimism and excitement about the future.

2. A preference or tendency to think in "big picture" terms, as opposed to concentrating on minute details and micromanaging issues.

3. An outlook that values individuals for their unique talents and seeks to maximize their self-actualization as the building blocks of organizational success.

To what extent can such leadership qualities be acquired? Can anyone *learn* to be a leader? Psychologists currently disagree so much about how to define leadership in the first place that the issue of its personality basis is quite secondary. For example, would it be accurate to define all Fortune 500 CEOs as leaders and then find out their shared personality traits? How about all one hundred United States senators or all living Nobel-prize-winning scientists? Aren't they clearly leaders in their own fields? As you can see, the conceptual waters get muddy very quickly. Nevertheless, major companies are probably rightfully concerned about fostering true leadership for the years ahead—if only within the context of their own organization or industry.

Before tackling the sample personality tests that focus on *leadership,* here are the three hiring zones that emanate from testing, and which, for job recruiters, meaningfully differentiate among candidates:

Definitely Hire:

This person shows definite leadership ability. She views the future as exciting and dynamic and likes to think in visionary terms. She is disposed to emphasize the strengths of others, rather than their weaknesses. She feels that empowering others makes for organizational success.

Maybe Hire:

This person shows some leadership ability. She is generally optimistic and excited about the future and likes to think in visionary terms. She is usually disposed to emphasize the strengths of others, rather than their weaknesses. She feels that empowering others often makes for organizational success.

Definitely Do Not Hire:

This person does not show leadership ability. She is pessimistic and even gloomy about the future. She believes that thinking in visionary terms is unproductive. She is disposed to emphasize the weaknesses of others, rather than their strengths. She feels that empowering others undermines organizational success.

Sample Test Questions

It's increasingly likely today that any personality test you take during the hiring process—especially for a management-track position—will include a scale aimed at measuring your leadership ability. To help you master this scale, three sample tests—each containing thirty questions—follows. Be aware, though, that in the real-life situation such questions will invariably be interspersed throughout the overall personality test you'll be taking and will definitely not appear consecutively or even grouped close together. Afterward, in the scoring procedure typically hidden from the candidate, his or her responses on this scale are tabulated and an overall score is generated, together with its interpretation for the hiring entity.

TEST OF LEADERSHIP #1

1. I believe that most people receive adequate respect at work.
2. The majority of people are already inspired to do their best at work.

> *A hallmark of leadership today is viewed as the ability to inspire others, so* strongly disagree *is the response that shows appropriate interest.*

3. Nothing motivates employees more than money or fear of losing their job.

> *The opposite of the enlightened leader is to support this statement; therefore,* strongly disagree *is the relevant reply.*

4. Every person has a potential to be creative at work.

> *A key value of leadership today is to voice this sentiment, so* strongly agree *is the fitting reply.*

5. When people are challenged creatively at work, they usually become more productive.

> *This statement is likewise a basic element in enlightened leadership philosophy today; thus,* strongly agree *is the appropriate answer.*

6. Every employee should be treated with dignity.
7. Employees who dislike their work are often highly productive.
8. It's rare that employees are adequately motivated by their boss.
9. To motivate employees, you must offer them a big goal they can support.
10. It's possible for a company to get so concerned about details that it falls apart.
11. There's something odd about people who think about the future a lot.
12. To be a success in life, you've got to think at least five or ten years into the future.
13. The great figures in history always looked at least five or ten years into the future.

> *Another recognized feature of leadership today is the ability to make effective long-range plans. Thus,* strongly agree *is the fitting reply.*

14. Life is a lot more boring than most people will admit.

> *Leaders, like entrepreneurs, are never bored. They would therefore* strongly disagree *with this sentiment.*

15. It's always individual people who make history.
16. People are either born successful or not.

17. People can become successful through inspiration.

18. Good teachers are overrated in how much they affect their students.

19. I dislike managers who fail to give praise to their employees.

20. It's rare to see someone really excited about his or her work.

21. I don't recall the last time I praised a coworker's achievement.

22. There's too much criticism and not enough praise in the workplace today.

23. The most successful people are those who have been inspired by a big idea or goal.

> *The leadership literature nowadays is filled*
> *with anecdotes about inspiring employees*
> *to work toward a big, visionary goal. So,*
> *the relevant response is to strongly agree*
> *with this statement.*

24. Basically, people just want to get through each day with a minimum of hassles.

25. Boredom is always caused by a failure to excite one's imagination.

26. I'm always thinking about new ideas and ways that could improve our world.

27. To inspire people, you have to be inspired yourself.

28. I have a strong set of personal goals.

29. I usually get bored lounging around on a vacation and quickly want to get back to work.

30. There's something weak about people who think a lot about their upcoming vacation.

TEST OF LEADERSHIP #2

1. In my opinion, most people aren't inspired to achieve to their full potential.

2. I don't believe that people receive enough respect at work.

3. Regardless of what experts might say, I know that most people want to work hard.

4. I admire a person who gets a group excited and energized.

5. There's no such thing as leadership in business.

6. It must be admitted that most people are not very creative.

7. When people are challenged creatively at work, they often develop new ideas and methods.

8. Employees who enjoy their work a lot sometimes become less productive as a result.

9. It's not true that happier employees have less absenteeism.

10. To motivate employees, you must make them fear job loss or demotion.

   *Again, enlightened leadership today rejects
   such "lower values" thinking; thus, to
   strongly disagree is the relevant answer.*

11. The problem with most companies is that their bosses think too much about the "big picture."

12. It's not true that big goals count for more than little achievements in making a successful company.

13. People who think about the future a lot are usually high achievers.

14. To be a success in life, you've got to ignore the future as best as you can.

15. The great figures in history have always focused on the present rather than the future.

16. I doubt that most people are waiting to be inspired by somebody or something.

17. No matter what we may hear, there are very few exciting new things happening in the world.

18. Work can be much more interesting than the way most people experience it.

19. People really have much less control over their lives than they think.

   *Another trait of leadership is considered to be a
   strong sense of personal control over one's
   life; therefore, to strongly disagree is the
   fitting answer.*

20. People become more successful when they are properly motivated.

21. A good teacher can have a great effect on his/her students.

22. I find that too many people fritter away their lives on trivial things.

23. Most employees respond better to criticism than to praise.

24. Basically, people at work want to get a feeling of inspiration each day.

25. Boredom is basic to human nature.

26. Most managers don't give enough praise to employees.

27. I rarely have a strong set of personal goals.

   *Leaders, almost by definition, possess a strong
   set of personal goals. So, to strongly
   disagree is the appropriate answer.*

28. I have rarely met anyone who seemed inspired by his or her work.

29. There's nothing like lounging around on a vacation to make you feel alive.

> *Leaders aren't supposed to crave vacations, so to* strongly disagree *is the appropriate response.*

30. With better leadership, many companies would achieve more productivity and profitability.

> *The business books are filled with affirmations that dynamic leadership can transform virtually any enterprise. So, to* strongly agree *is the consistent reply.*

TEST OF LEADERSHIP #3

1. I disagree that most people receive adequate respect at work.
2. Most people are inspired to do their best at work.
3. Nothing motivates employees to work harder than money or fear of losing their job.
4. Every person has a big potential to be creative at work.
5. When people are challenged creatively at work, they almost always become more productive.
6. Every employee should be treated with kindness.
7. Employees who dislike their work are rarely highly productive.
8. It's very rare for employees to be adequately motivated by their boss.
9. To inspire employees, you must offer them a big goal they can endorse.
10. It's common for companies to get so concerned about details that they fall apart.

> *An axiom among enlightened leadership thinkers today is that micromanagement is destructive; so, to* strongly agree *is the appropriate answer.*

11. There's something strange about people who think about the future a lot.
12. To be a success in life, you've certainly got to think at least five or ten years into the future.
13. The great shapers of history always looked at least five or ten years into the future.
14. Life is often tedious.
15. It's always individuals, not impersonal social forces, that make history.
16. Some people are just born to be successful.

17. People can become more successful through the right motivation.

    Enlightened leadership stresses that training
    and experience, not innate qualities, create
    more productive employees. Thus,
    strongly agree is the fitting reply.

18. Teachers are often overrated in how much they can affect their students.

19. I strongly dislike managers who don't praise their employees.

20. It's very rare to see someone truly excited about his or her work.

21. I can't recall the last time I criticized a coworker.

22. I don't believe there's too much criticism and not enough praise in the workplace today.

23. Generally, successful people are those who have been inspired by a big idea or goal.

24. I dislike people who just want to get through each day with nothing more than a minimum of hassles.

25. Boredom is usually caused by a failure to excite one's imagination.

26. I often think about new ideas and ways that could improve our world.

    Like entrepreneurs, leaders are extolled for
    their innovativeness. Thus, to strongly
    agree shows you have the right stuff.

27. To inspire people, you must feel inspired yourself.

28. I have always had a strong set of personal goals.

29. I sometimes get bored lounging around on a vacation and quickly want to get back to work.

30. No matter what the leadership, most companies perform about the same depending on external, market conditions.

14
Beating Test Jitters

While taking a personality test to learn more about yourself can be an enjoyable—even fascinating—experience, it's likely to arouse anxiety when it's part of the hiring process. After all, not only are you revealing private feelings, attitudes, and goals to a total stranger, but your own statements may well make or break your job candidacy. What sensible person wouldn't get at least a little rattled in this situation? So, first of all, you're perfectly normal if the thought of submitting to detailed questions about your inner world is making you worry. But remember, essentially the test is seeking to assess you in these seven specific areas: conscientiousness, extraversion, integrity, anger, entrepreneurialism, stress tolerance, and leadership. It's improbable that other aspects of your personality will be deeply probed, and rest assured, questions about your sexuality violate federal and state laws, and will definitely not be asked. As indicated earlier in this book, though, you have almost no legal protection about what happens to your answers once you turn them in; so all the more reason to be as clear-headed as possible before responding.

Over the years, I've taught stress reduction to countless individuals facing anxiety-evoking circumstances. Here are seven proven methods for staying calm and composed during the interview and standardized test procedures:

1. Get a Good Night's Sleep.

Psychologists now know that your mother was right: If you get less than adequate sleep, your mental functioning and alertness the following day will definitely diminish. Lately, researchers have been commenting that Americans are a "sleep-deprived society," with millions of individual adults and teens suffering chronically, with symptoms of tiredness, irritability, memory loss, and poor concentration from such deprivation. But I'm not asking you here to change society; only that in your own case, make sure that prior to the evaluation, you've had adequate rest the night before. For most of us, this means a solid eight to nine hours of sleep.

2. Don't Take Medication Before the Test Unless It's Absolutely Necessary for Your Health.

If you suffer from asthma or high blood pressure, then of course you must take your medicine. But if it's a matter of pills for mild allergies or weight reduction, be aware that many types of medication adversely affect our ability to concentrate, focus, and maintain attention. Because it's so vital to be maximally alert during the test and interview (yawning in the face of your potential employer is never help-ful), it might be worthwhile to suspend such nonessential medicine for the day.

3. This May Seem Obvious, but I'll Say It Anyway: Do Not Ingest Either Liquor or Recreational Drugs.

I'm not here to lecture you about the morality of your lifestyle, but you ought to know that both liquor and recreational drugs severely impair your cognitive abil-ities. And here's a helpful insight: Interviewers aren't favorably disposed to can-didates who come in with liquor on their breath or with either bloodshot or spaced-out eyes. The time to have a pleasant drink is not before your test (or inter-view), but afterward.

4. Eat a Nutritious Breakfast.

Specifically, this means to avoid high-sugar foods like doughnuts and pastries, which will cause your alertness suddenly to plummet once they're absorbed into your bloodstream. Instead, consume a high-carbohydrate meal, such as hot cereal, cold cereal, toast or bagel. This will release sugars into your bloodstream at a much slower, more even pace. If a cup, or two, of coffee or caffeinated tea helps charge you physically, now isn't the time to become a health-food advo-cate. Just go light on the sugar.

5. Know That Mild Anxiety Actually Improves Your Test Performance.

That's right, surprising as it may seem, psychologists have found that of the three possible conditions—no tension, mild tension, and severe tension—people with mild tension do better than their counterparts in the other two situations. In a way, this makes sense: If you're too relaxed, you may become physically drowsy or mentally indifferent to how you're doing on the test. So be glad that you actually feel mildly nervous; it will sharpen your focus.

6. What If Your Jitters Aren't So Mild? What If You're Starting to Worry As You Sit Down to the Interview or Standardized Test?

This is a different matter entirely from mild tension. At all costs, you want to prevent feelings of panic from arising and swirling, because panic can totally ruin your concentration and emotional stability. If you start to get quite nervous, here's a useful exercise to do immediately:

Close your eyes and purse your lips. Breathe in and out evenly through your nostrils. Now, bring your awareness to the exact point where the air enters your nostrils. Keep focusing on that point. Next, picture a scene in your mind's eye that is especially relaxing for you: perhaps lying on the beach on a dazzling summer's morning, or walking along a forest path on a bright autumn afternoon, or sitting before a crackling fireplace in a cozy living room on a mellow winter's evening. Certainly, you can picture a friend or loved one with you. As you mentally hold the image, feel a sense of well-being and calmness pervade your being. Feel better? Just remember, you don't want to get too calm—as previously explained.

7. Adopt a Positive Attitude.

Psychologists have found that what we tell ourselves inwardly is very important for our mental health. So it's advisable to take the perspective that the interview and standardized test are all part of a learning experience for you, and that regardless of the outcome for a particular job opening, you're gaining valuable lessons in taking tests and responding to interviews more effectively. If, conversely, you find yourself saying negative things like, "I'm going to mess up, I just know it," then stop the train of thoughts immediately by thinking about a time in which you showed high achievement or won praise for your accomplishments. Now focus on that feeling of self-esteem and let it expand inside you.

There are probably a hundred more snippets of advice that I, or others, could give you. But they wouldn't add much to these pointers and might even prove confusing and contradictory. Therefore, bearing these guidelines in mind, you're now ready to take the first practice personality test.

PART 3
Six Sample Personality Tests

Test-Taking Instructions

For Sample Personality Tests 1 through 6

Please read these instructions before starting. Use a number 2 pencil to mark you answers in the spaces indicated. DO NOT write in the book.

This questionnaire comprises ninety statements. Please read each one carefully and fill in the one answer that best corresponds to your agreement or disagreement.

Fill in *SD* if the statement is definitely false or if you **strongly disagree.**

Fill in *D* if the statement is mostly false or if you **disagree.**

Fill in *N* if the statement is about equally true or false, if you cannot decide, or if you are **neutral** on the statement.

Fill in *A* if the statement is mostly true or if you **agree.**

Fill in *SA* if the statement is definitely true or if you **strongly agree.**

There are no right or wrong answers, and you need not be an "expert" to finish this questionnaire. Describe yourself honestly and state your opinions as accurately as possible.

Answer every item and be sure to fill in the circles completely. Please make sure that your response is marked in the correct space. If you make a mistake or change your mind, erase your first answer completely. Then fill in the circle that corresponds to your correct answer.

SAMPLE PERSONALITY TEST #1

1. I have an unhurried attitude toward work and play.   ○ SD   ○ D   ○ N   ○ A   ○ SA

2. I generally stay away from crowds.   ○ SD   ○ D   ○ N   ○ A   ○ SA

3. As a student, I excelled in everything.   ○ SD   ○ D   ○ N   ○ A   ○ SA

4. Everyone loses their temper at work sometimes.   ○ SD   ○ D   ○ N   ○ A   ○ SA

5. I believe that most people are honest.   ○ SD   ○ D   ○ N   ○ A   ○ SA

6. I prefer to follow established routines at work.   ○ SD   ○ D   ○ N   ○ A   ○ SA

7. I do not worry a lot.   ○ SD   ○ D   ○ N   ○ A   ○ SA

8. Thinking about the future excites me.   ○ SD   ○ D   ○ N   ○ A   ○ SA

9. I try to finish all the tasks given to me.   ○ SD   ○ D   ○ N   ○ A   ○ SA

10. I don't enjoy chatting with others very much.   ○ SD   ○ D   ○ N   ○ A   ○ SA

11. Sometimes my anger jumps out of me.   ○ SD   ○ D   ○ N   ○ A   ○ SA

12. People usually act from good motives.   ○ SD   ○ D   ○ N   ○ A   ○ SA

13. I ponder things carefully before making a decision.   ○ SD   ○ D   ○ N   ○ A   ○ SA

14. I frequently feel unable to function due to stress.   ○ SD   ○ D   ○ N   ○ A   ○ SA

15. Most workers would prefer to do as little as possible.   ○ SD   ○ D   ○ N   ○ A   ○ SA

16. I have never acted on an impulse.   ○ SD   ○ D   ○ N   ○ A   ○ SA

17. I have never read a boring book.   ○ SD   ○ D   ○ N   ○ A   ○ SA

18. I keep my work area as tidy as possible.   ○ SD   ○ D   ○ N   ○ A   ○ SA

19. I generally prefer to do things by myself.   ○ SD   ○ D   ○ N   ○ A   ○ SA

20. Hotheaded people should not be hired for most jobs.   ○ SD   ○ D   ○ N   ○ A   ○ SA

21. Parents are obligated to train their children to be honest.   ○ SD   ○ D   ○ N   ○ A   ○ SA

22. I get bored easily with routines.   ○ SD   ○ D   ○ N   ○ A   ○ SA

23. I seldom feel afraid or worried.   ○ SD   ○ D   ○ N   ○ A   ○ SA

24. Most people are out for themselves.   ○ SD   ○ D   ○ N   ○ A   ○ SA

25. I am not a very organized individual.   ○ SD   ○ D   ○ N   ○ A   ○ SA

26. Crowds sometimes make me tense.   ○ SD   ○ D   ○ N   ○ A   ○ SA

27. People who are angry a lot have a big problem.   ○ SD   ○ D   ○ N   ○ A   ○ SA

28. There is too much dishonesty in the workplace.   ○ SD   ○ D   ○ N   ○ A   ○ SA

29. I believe that taking risks is a key to success.   ○ SD   ○ D   ○ N   ○ A   ○ SA

30. Frequently, I feel nervous.   ○ SD   ○ D   ○ N   ○ A   ○ SA

31. People are often not challenged enough at work.   ○ SD   ○ D   ○ N   ○ A   ○ SA

32. I am known to be highly effective at work.   ○ SD   ○ D   ○ N   ○ A   ○ SA

33. If I am alone for a while, I feel a strong need for company. ○ SD ○ D ○ N ○ A ○ SA

34. I never disliked a teacher. ○ SD ○ D ○ N ○ A ○ SA

35. Nobody has a right to get angry on the job. ○ SD ○ D ○ N ○ A ○ SA

36. An employee who is caught stealing should be fired immediately. ○ SD ○ D ○ N ○ A ○ SA

37. The thought of starting my own business appeals to me. ○ SD ○ D ○ N ○ A ○ SA

38. My friends consider me a little overly sensitive. ○ SD ○ D ○ N ○ A ○ SA

39. Most people enjoy challenges at work. ○ SD ○ D ○ N ○ A ○ SA

40. I often enter into situations without enough preparation. ○ SD ○ D ○ N ○ A ○ SA

41. I have recently been at some great parties. ○ SD ○ D ○ N ○ A ○ SA

42. I used to lose my temper a lot. ○ SD ○ D ○ N ○ A ○ SA

43. I think nearly everyone has occasionally been tempted to steal. ○ SD ○ D ○ N ○ A ○ SA

44. I enjoy trying new tastes and foods. ○ SD ○ D ○ N ○ A ○ SA

45. I am "cool as a cucumber" in emergencies. ○ SD ○ D ○ N ○ A ○ SA

46. I am not a very optimistic person. ○ SD ○ D ○ N ○ A ○ SA

47. I strive to accomplish all my goals. ○ SD ○ D ○ N ○ A ○ SA

48. I like to be around people while waiting in a bus or train station. ○ SD ○ D ○ N ○ A ○ SA

49. I rarely feel angry at work. ○ SD ○ D ○ N ○ A ○ SA

50. At times, I cheat when playing cards by myself. ○ SD ○ D ○ N ○ A ○ SA

51. Sometimes, people who take risks are inviting disaster. ○ SD ○ D ○ N ○ A ○ SA

52. I have sometimes had trouble falling asleep due to work stress. ○ SD ○ D ○ N ○ A ○ SA

53. Everyone has a potential to accomplish more in life. ○ SD ○ D ○ N ○ A ○ SA

54. I never turned in a homework assignment late. ○ SD ○ D ○ N ○ A ○ SA

55. I enjoy finding answers to problems. ○ SD ○ D ○ N ○ A ○ SA

56. Sometimes I am really happy just being by myself. ○ SD ○ D ○ N ○ A ○ SA

57. An employee who is angry a lot should get counseling or be fired. ○ SD ○ D ○ N ○ A ○ SA

58. Teachers should not tolerate a student who cheats on exams. ○ SD ○ D ○ N ○ A ○ SA

59. The people I admire most have usually been risk-takers. ○ SD ○ D ○ N ○ A ○ SA

60. I have sometimes felt like crying because of work problems. ○ SD ○ D ○ N ○ A ○ SA

61. I have headed groups I've belonged to. ○ SD ○ D ○ N ○ A ○ SA

62. I like to finish tasks on time. ○ SD ○ D ○ N ○ A ○ SA

63. Loud parties sometimes drain me. ○ SD ○ D ○ N ○ A ○ SA

64. Losing your temper is a sign of personal weakness. ○ SD ○ D ○ N ○ A ○ SA

65. Most teenagers have shoplifted at least once. ○ SD ○ D ○ N ○ A ○ SA

66. Before I act, I want to have all the information I need. ○ SD ○ D ○ N ○ A ○ SA

67. I wish I could handle stress better at work. ○ SD ○ D ○ N ○ A ○ SA

68. At meetings, people often look to me for guidance. ○ SD ○ D ○ N ○ A ○ SA

69. I sometimes find it hard to set priorities at work. ○ SD ○ D ○ N ○ A ○ SA

70. I like to make small talk with people I don't know well. ○ SD ○ D ○ N ○ A ○ SA

71. I've always had the perfect job. ○ SD ○ D ○ N ○ A ○ SA

72. I have sometimes felt like getting even with a coworker who insulted me. ○ SD ○ D ○ N ○ A ○ SA

73. Parents should punish their children who are caught stealing at school. ○ SD ○ D ○ N ○ A ○ SA

74. I like to trust my intuition a lot. ○ SD ○ D ○ N ○ A ○ SA

75. I have sometimes had a stomach problem due to work tension. ○ SD ○ D ○ N ○ A ○ SA

76. Thinking about big goals in life excites me. ○ SD ○ D ○ N ○ A ○ SA

77. I rarely leave a job undone. ○ SD ○ D ○ N ○ A ○ SA

78. Loud parties really get me in a happy mood. ○ SD ○ D ○ N ○ A ○ SA

79. Everybody has thought about harming his or her boss. ○ SD ○ D ○ N ○ A ○ SA

80. Our society's laws are too lenient about shoplifting. ○ SD ○ D ○ N ○ A ○ SA

81. You can't succeed in business without taking risks. ○ SD ○ D ○ N ○ A ○ SA

82. I never eat too much due to stress. ○ SD ○ D ○ N ○ A ○ SA

83. I would prefer to just go my own way at work. ○ SD ○ D ○ N ○ A ○ SA

84. I don't mind staying late at work to get a task done. ○ SD ○ D ○ N ○ A ○ SA

85. I like to unwind by laughing loudly with a group. ○ SD ○ D ○ N ○ A ○ SA

86. I must admit that I have lost my temper at a coworker who annoyed me. ○ SD ○ D ○ N ○ A ○ SA

87. I admire parents who are stern in disciplining their children never to steal. ○ SD ○ D ○ N ○ A ○ SA

88. My friends would agree that I have excellent intuition. ○ SD ○ D ○ N ○ A ○ SA

89. I have sometimes felt like quitting a job due to tension. ○ SD ○ D ○ N ○ A ○ SA

90. I want to be remembered for having achieved great things. ○ SD ○ D ○ N ○ A ○ SA

YOUR TEST RESULTS: PERSONALITY TEST #1

Scoring Method:

Strongly Disagree = 1, Disagree = 2, Neutral = 3, Agree = 4, Strongly Agree = 5

Lie Scale:

Add your scores for questions 3, 16, 17, 34, 54, 71.   TOTAL _____

> If your total score = 30, the alarm bell is screeching.
> If your total score is 24 to 29, the alarm is loud.
> If your total score is 19 to 23, the alarm is soft but clear.
> If your total score is 18 or lower, the alarm is silent.

1. *Conscientiousness*

Add your scores for questions 9, 18, 32, 47, 55, 62, 69, 77, 84.   TOTAL _____

Subtract your scores for questions 1, 25, 40.   TOTAL _____

Record your total score: TOTAL _____

> Total score = 29 or lower
>
> > You're not conscientious enough for anyone to hire you. Change your attitude, quick.
>
> Total score = 30 to 32
>
> > Unless you get lucky, you have too little conscientiousness to be hired. Change your attitude.
>
> Total score = 33 to 35
>
> > You probably are conscientious enough to be hired—as long as there's a tight hiring market.
>
> Total score = 36 to 41
>
> > Your high conscientiousness will endear you to employers.
>
> Total score = 42
>
> > You're so conscientious that your employers will hold you up as a role model.

2. *Extraversion*

Add your scores for questions 33, 41, 48, 70, 78, 85.   **TOTAL** _____

Subtract your scores for questions 2, 10, 19, 26, 56, 63.   **TOTAL** _____

Record your total score: **TOTAL** _____

Total score = 11 or lower

You're definitely an introvert and would be better off in appropriate jobs.

Total score = 12 to 17

You're on the introverted side and would be best suited for such jobs.

Total score = 18 to 21

You're probably extraverted enough to get hired for most jobs.

Total score = 22 to 23

You're definitely on the extraverted side, and employers will recognize that.

Total score = 24

You're highly extraverted and will be valued as such by employers.

3. *Integrity*

Add your scores for questions 5, 12, 21, 28, 36, 58, 73, 80, 87.   **TOTAL** _____

Subtract your scores for questions 43, 50, 65.   **TOTAL** _____

Record your total score: **TOTAL** _____

Total score = 29 or lower

You're too low on integrity to be hired by anybody. A change of heart could help you a lot.

Total score = 30 to 32

You're too low on integrity to attract employers. A change of heart would help.

Total score = 33 to 35

You've probably too little integrity to be hired by many employers. Change a few things in your outlook.

Total score = 36 to 41

You've enough integrity to be hired by most employers.

Total score = 42

You're a person of high integrity, or at least one who tests out that way. Employers will definitely want you.

4. *Anger*

Add your scores for questions 20, 27, 35, 49, 57, 64.   **TOTAL** _____

Subtract your scores for questions 4, 11, 42, 72, 79, 86.   **TOTAL** _____

Record your total score: **TOTAL** _____

Total score = 11 or lower

You're a potential eruption in the workplace. Get professional help, quick.

Total score = 12 to 17

You've got too much anger to be hired. Get professional help, the sooner the better.

Total score = 18 to 21

You've probably too much anger to be hired. Professional help might be a good idea.

Total score = 22 to 23

You're low enough on anger to be hired.

Total score = 24

You're a low-anger person, and employers will value that.

5. *Entrepreneurialism*

Add your scores for questions 22, 29, 37, 44, 59, 74, 81, 88.   **TOTAL** _____

Subtract your scores for questions 6, 13, 51, 66.   **TOTAL** _____

Record your total score: **TOTAL** _____

Total score = 23 or lower

You definitely don't have the entrepreneurial personality. But you didn't really want to start a business, did you?

Total score = 24 to 27

You don't have the ingredients for entrepreneurship, but that shouldn't surprise you.

Total score = 28 to 31

Your entrepreneurialism may be adequate to entice employers.

Total score = 32 to 35

You have entrepreneurial talent sought by employers.

Total score = 36

You have plenty of entrepreneurial talent. Go for it.

6. *Stress Tolerance*

Add your scores for questions 7, 23, 45, 82.   TOTAL _____

Subtract your scores for questions 14, 30, 38, 52, 60, 67, 75, 89.   TOTAL _____

Record your total score: TOTAL _____

Total score = below 0

Your poor ability to handle stress will turn away employers. Stress-management training would be useful.

Total score = 0 to 4

Your meager ability to handle stress won't attract employers. Stress-management training would be useful.

Total score = 5 to 7

Your ability to handle stress may be adequate to get hired.

Total score = 8 to 11

Your good ability to handle stress will be recognized by employers.

Total score = 12

Your excellent ability to handle stress will be prized by employers.

7. *Leadership*

Add your scores for questions 8, 31, 39, 53, 61, 68, 76, 90.   TOTAL _____

Subtract your scores for questions 15, 24, 46, 83.   TOTAL _____

Your total score: TOTAL _____

Total score = 23 or lower

You have minimal leadership ability. Sorry, that's a fact.

Total score = 24 to 27

You don't have enough leadership ability to attract employers.

Total score = 28 to 31

You have adequate leadership ability for some employers, especially in a tight hiring market.

Total score = 32 to 35

Your leadership ability is apparent and will be recognized by employers.

Total score = 36

Your high leadership ability will be prized. Use it well.

SAMPLE PERSONALITY TEST #2

1. Many of my friends would describe me as quick-tempered. ○ SD ○ D ○ N ○ A ○ SA

2. I would like the challenge of starting my own business. ○ SD ○ D ○ N ○ A ○ SA

3. I try to accomplish everything I am given to do. ○ SD ○ D ○ N ○ A ○ SA

4. I never fret about matters in my life. ○ SD ○ D ○ N ○ A ○ SA

5. People who know me regard me as extremely honest. ○ SD ○ D ○ N ○ A ○ SA

6. I am generally suspicious of other people's intentions. ○ SD ○ D ○ N ○ A ○ SA

7. I enjoy the company of most people. ○ SD ○ D ○ N ○ A ○ SA

8. I often get angry at people I know. ○ SD ○ D ○ N ○ A ○ SA

9. Once I learn something a certain way, I like to do it that way. ○ SD ○ D ○ N ○ A ○ SA

10. I find it hard to keep at self-improvement programs. ○ SD ○ D ○ N ○ A ○ SA

11. I am a relaxed person and handle change well. ○ SD ○ D ○ N ○ A ○ SA

12. I don't think that most teenagers have shoplifted at least once. ○ SD ○ D ○ N ○ A ○ SA

13. Only a few people can be better motivated to achieve their best. ○ SD ○ D ○ N ○ A ○ SA

14. I usually avoid becoming part of a crowd. ○ SD ○ D ○ N ○ A ○ SA

15. I often get mad about how others treat me. ○ SD ○ D ○ N ○ A ○ SA

16. I enjoy having lots of options. ○ SD ○ D ○ N ○ A ○ SA

17. I'm certainly not the most organized person who has ever lived. ○ SD ○ D ○ N ○ A ○ SA

18. I feel the workday is too short to accomplish what I need to. ○ SD ○ D ○ N ○ A ○ SA

19. I would rather have an honest friend than a devoted one. ○ SD ○ D ○ N ○ A ○ SA

20. I have rarely been asked to lead a meeting at work. ○ SD ○ D ○ N ○ A ○ SA

21. I hate being alone. ○ SD ○ D ○ N ○ A ○ SA

22. I have never yelled at a coworker. ○ SD ○ D ○ N ○ A ○ SA

23. I trust my intuition almost all the time. ○ SD ○ D ○ N ○ A ○ SA

24. I keep my workspace tidy and neat. ○ SD ○ D ○ N ○ A ○ SA

25. I often feel high pressure at work. ○ SD ○ D ○ N ○ A ○ SA

26. Honesty is not always the best policy in business. ○ SD ○ D ○ N ○ A ○ SA

27. Most people have a big potential for accomplishment.   ○ SD   ○ D   ○ N   ○ A   ○ SA

28. I don't like to chat with strangers on a bus or plane.   ○ SD   ○ D   ○ N   ○ A   ○ SA

29. I have never been annoyed with a coworker.   ○ SD   ○ D   ○ N   ○ A   ○ SA

30. I hate taking risks.   ○ SD   ○ D   ○ N   ○ A   ○ SA

31. I have never had a disagreement with anyone at work.   ○ SD   ○ D   ○ N   ○ A   ○ SA

32. I have failed to finish a task at work because I felt worried.   ○ SD   ○ D   ○ N   ○ A   ○ SA

33. I have sometimes called in sick just to take a day off and relax.   ○ SD   ○ D   ○ N   ○ A   ○ SA

34. People can achieve more when they have an exciting goal.   ○ SD   ○ D   ○ N   ○ A   ○ SA

35. I like the presence of others around me.   ○ SD   ○ D   ○ N   ○ A   ○ SA

36. Parents should certainly discipline children who get angry a lot.   ○ SD   ○ D   ○ N   ○ A   ○ SA

37. The thought of starting my own business is unappealing.   ○ SD   ○ D   ○ N   ○ A   ○ SA

38. I sometimes lose my focus in the middle of the workday.   ○ SD   ○ D   ○ N   ○ A   ○ SA

39. I have rarely had a headache due to work tension.   ○ SD   ○ D   ○ N   ○ A   ○ SA

40. Employees have no right to take home any supplies.   ○ SD   ○ D   ○ N   ○ A   ○ SA

41. I want to lead people as one of my chief goals.   ○ SD   ○ D   ○ N   ○ A   ○ SA

42. I usually prefer to do things alone.   ○ SD   ○ D   ○ N   ○ A   ○ SA

43. I would not keep a friend who lost his or her temper frequently at work.   ○ SD   ○ D   ○ N   ○ A   ○ SA

44. I enjoy making decisions when all the information is not available.   ○ SD   ○ D   ○ N   ○ A   ○ SA

45. I can fritter away the hours rather easily at work.   ○ SD   ○ D   ○ N   ○ A   ○ SA

46. I sometimes have trouble sleeping due to work tensions.   ○ SD   ○ D   ○ N   ○ A   ○ SA

47. I would report a coworker who had called in sick and then gone shopping for the day.   ○ SD   ○ D   ○ N   ○ A   ○ SA

48. I like to take charge in large meetings.   ○ SD   ○ D   ○ N   ○ A   ○ SA

49. I have often gotten really bored at parties.   ○ SD   ○ D   ○ N   ○ A   ○ SA

50. People who get angry a lot should get counseling.   ○ SD   ○ D   ○ N   ○ A   ○ SA

51. I usually like to start new projects where the outcome is uncertain.   ○ SD   ○ D   ○ N   ○ A   ○ SA

52. I am not very tidy in my living space.   ○ SD   ○ D   ○ N   ○ A   ○ SA

53. I find it hard to unwind after work due to stress.   ○ SD   ○ D   ○ N   ○ A   ○ SA

54. Shoplifting is really something normal for most
    teenagers to do.   ○ SD   ○ D   ○ N   ○ A   ○ SA

55. I want to be in charge of a big project and involve
    others in it.   ○ SD   ○ D   ○ N   ○ A   ○ SA

56. At parties, I prefer to let others introduce themselves
    to me, rather than introduce myself first.   ○ SD   ○ D   ○ N   ○ A   ○ SA

57. I have never driven a car above the posted speed limit.   ○ SD   ○ D   ○ N   ○ A   ○ SA

58. At work, I have sometimes felt like hitting the wall in
    anger.   ○ SD   ○ D   ○ N   ○ A   ○ SA

59. Risk-takers are often big failures.   ○ SD   ○ D   ○ N   ○ A   ○ SA

60. I strive to meet my goals in life.   ○ SD   ○ D   ○ N   ○ A   ○ SA

61. I often feel scared about failing at work.   ○ SD   ○ D   ○ N   ○ A   ○ SA

62. Our society is too stern in punishing shoplifters.   ○ SD   ○ D   ○ N   ○ A   ○ SA

63. I seldom like to take charge in a meeting.   ○ SD   ○ D   ○ N   ○ A   ○ SA

64. Some of my best times have been when I'm alone.   ○ SD   ○ D   ○ N   ○ A   ○ SA

65. People should never feel justified in yelling at work.   ○ SD   ○ D   ○ N   ○ A   ○ SA

66. I like to try new restaurants just for the fun of it.   ○ SD   ○ D   ○ N   ○ A   ○ SA

67. There's nothing wrong with resting during work now
    and then.   ○ SD   ○ D   ○ N   ○ A   ○ SA

68. I have sometimes been unable to stop thinking about
    a problem at work.   ○ SD   ○ D   ○ N   ○ A   ○ SA

69. I've never called in sick unless I was really unable to
    work.   ○ SD   ○ D   ○ N   ○ A   ○ SA

70. My friends would describe me as having leadership
    ability.   ○ SD   ○ D   ○ N   ○ A   ○ SA

71. I really dislike having to spend time by myself.   ○ SD   ○ D   ○ N   ○ A   ○ SA

72. I have never lost a night's sleep worrying about
    something.   ○ SD   ○ D   ○ N   ○ A   ○ SA

73. There is no excuse to lose your temper at work.   ○ SD   ○ D   ○ N   ○ A   ○ SA

74. It's usually better to stick with what you've mastered
    than to try new ways of solving problems.   ○ SD   ○ D   ○ N   ○ A   ○ SA

75. I don't mind working on a weekend if that's what is
    needed to finish a job on time.   ○ SD   ○ D   ○ N   ○ A   ○ SA

76. I have never been tired at work.   ○ SD   ○ D   ○ N   ○ A   ○ SA

77. It's ridiculous to say that honesty is always the best
    policy.   ○ SD   ○ D   ○ N   ○ A   ○ SA

78. I like to think about the future.   ○ SD   ○ D   ○ N   ○ A   ○ SA

79. I prefer a small quiet social event to a noisy party.   ○ SD   ○ D   ○ N   ○ A   ○ SA

80. No work assignment has ever bored me.   ○ SD   ○ D   ○ N   ○ A   ○ SA

81. Companies should have zero tolerance for employees
who lose their temper.   ○ SD   ○ D   ○ N   ○ A   ○ SA

82. The most successful business people have been very
willing to take risks.   ○ SD   ○ D   ○ N   ○ A   ○ SA

83. Sometimes working hard really gives you no payoff.   ○ SD   ○ D   ○ N   ○ A   ○ SA

84. My feelings get hurt easily if someone criticizes my
performance.   ○ SD   ○ D   ○ N   ○ A   ○ SA

85. All my friends are very trustworthy.   ○ SD   ○ D   ○ N   ○ A   ○ SA

86. Most people respond better to praise than to criticism.   ○ SD   ○ D   ○ N   ○ A   ○ SA

87. Some of my best times have been at big parties.   ○ SD   ○ D   ○ N   ○ A   ○ SA

88. I have never actually been lost.   ○ SD   ○ D   ○ N   ○ A   ○ SA

89. It would be false to say I worry too much.   ○ SD   ○ D   ○ N   ○ A   ○ SA

90. I work as hard as I can almost always.   ○ SD   ○ D   ○ N   ○ A   ○ SA

YOUR TEST RESULTS: SAMPLE TEST #2

Scoring Method:

Strongly Disagree = 1, Disagree = 2, Neutral = 3, Agree = 4, Strongly Agree = 5

Lie Scale:

Add your scores for questions 31, 57, 72, 76, 80, 88.   **TOTAL** _____

If your total score = 30, the alarm bell is screeching.

If your total score is 24 to 29, the alarm is loud.

If your total score is 19 to 23, the alarm is soft but clear.

If your total score is 18 or lower, the alarm is silent.

1. *Conscientiousness*

Add your scores for questions 3, 24, 60, 75, 90.   **TOTAL** _____

Subtract your scores for questions 10, 17, 38, 45, 52,
67, 83.   **TOTAL** _____

Your total score is: **TOTAL** _____

Total score = 5 or lower

You're not conscientious enough for anyone to hire you. Change your
attitude, quick.

Total score = 6 to 10

> Unless you get lucky, you have too little conscientiousness to be hired. Change your attitude.

Total score = 11 to 12

> You probably are conscientious enough to be hired—as long as there's a tight hiring market.

Total score = 13 to 17

> Your high conscientiousness will endear you to employers.

Total score = 18

> You're so conscientious that your employers will hold you up as a role model.

2. *Extraversion*

Add your scores for questions 7, 21, 35, 71, 87.   **TOTAL** _____

Subtract your scores for questions 14, 28, 42, 49, 56, 64, 79.   **TOTAL** _____

Your total score is: **TOTAL** _____

Total score = 5 or lower

> You're definitely an introvert and would be better off in appropriate jobs.

Total score = 6 to 10

> You're on the introverted side and would be best suited for such jobs.

Total score = 11 to 12

> You're probably extraverted enough to get hired for most jobs.

Total score = 13 to 17

> You're definitely on the extraverted side, and employers will recognize that.

Total score = 18

> You're highly extraverted and will be valued as such by employers.

3. *Integrity*

Add your scores for questions 5, 12, 19, 40, 47, 69, 85.   **TOTAL** _____

Subtract your scores for questions 26, 33, 54, 62, 77.   **TOTAL** _____

Your total score is: **TOTAL** _____

Total score = 17 or lower

> You're too low on integrity to be hired by anybody. A change of heart could help you a lot.

Total score = 18 to 22

You're too low on integrity to attract employers. A change of heart would help.

Total score = 23 to 24

You've probably too little integrity to be hired by many employers. Change a few things in your outlook.

Total score = 25 to 29

You've enough integrity to be hired by most employers.

Total score = 30

You're a person of high integrity, or at least one who tests out that way. Employers will definitely want you.

4. Anger

Add your scores for questions 22, 29, 36, 43, 50, 65, 73, 81.   **TOTAL** _____

Subtract your scores for questions 1, 8, 15, 58.   **TOTAL** _____

Your total score is: **TOTAL** _____

Total score = 23 or lower

You're a potential eruption in the workplace. Get professional help, quick.

Total score = 24 to 27

You've got too much anger to be hired. Get professional help, the sooner the better.

Total score = 28 to 31

You've probably too much anger to be hired. Professional help might be a good idea.

Total score = 32 to 35

You're low enough on anger to be hired.

Total score = 36

You're a low-anger person, and employers will value that.

5. Entrepreneurialism

Add your scores for questions 2, 16, 23, 44, 51, 66, 82.   **TOTAL** _____

Subtract your scores for questions 9, 30, 37, 59, 74.   **TOTAL** _____

Your total score is: **TOTAL** _____

Total score = 17 or lower

You definitely don't have the entrepreneurial personality. But you didn't really want to start a business, did you?

Total score = 18 to 22

You don't have the ingredients for entrepreneurship, but that shouldn't surprise you.

Total score = 23 to 24

Your entrepreneurialism may be adequate to entice employers.

Total score = 25 to 29

You have entrepreneurial talent sought by employers.

Total score = 30

You have plenty of entrepreneurial talent. Go for it.

6. *Stress Tolerance*

Add your scores for questions 4, 11, 39, 89   TOTAL _____

Subtract your scores for questions 18, 25, 32, 46, 53, 61,
68, 84.   TOTAL _____

Your total score is: TOTAL _____

Total score = below 0

Your poor ability to handle stress will turn away employers. Stress-management training would be useful.

Total score = 1 to 4

Your meager ability to handle stress won't attract employers. Stress-management training would be useful.

Total score = 5 to 7

Your ability to handle stress may be adequate to get hired.

Total score = 8 to 11

Your good ability to handle stress will be recognized by employers.

Total score = 12

Your excellent ability to handle stress will be prized by employers.

7. *Leadership*

Add your scores for questions 27, 34, 41, 48, 55, 70, 78, 86. TOTAL _____

Subtract your scores for questions 6, 13, 20, 63.   TOTAL _____

Your total score is: TOTAL _____

Total score = 23 or lower

You have minimal leadership ability. Sorry, that's a fact.

Total score = 24 to 27

You don't have enough leadership ability to attract employers.

Total score = 28 to 31

You have adequate leadership ability for some employers, especially in a tight hiring market.

Total score = 32 to 35

Your leadership ability is apparent and will be recognized by employers.

Total score = 36

Your high leadership ability will be prized. Use it well.

SAMPLE PERSONALITY TEST #3

1. I am considered a shy person.   ○ SD   ○ D   ○ N   ○ A   ○ SA

2. I have never disappointed anyone.   ○ SD   ○ D   ○ N   ○ A   ○ SA

3. I feel stressed-out a lot at work.   ○ SD   ○ D   ○ N   ○ A   ○ SA

4. I avoid situations where I have to lead a meeting.   ○ SD   ○ D   ○ N   ○ A   ○ SA

5. I would like to start a business in the next few years.   ○ SD   ○ D   ○ N   ○ A   ○ SA

6. I can't recall the last time I lost my temper at somebody.   ○ SD   ○ D   ○ N   ○ A   ○ SA

7. Honesty is among the most important values for me.   ○ SD   ○ D   ○ N   ○ A   ○ SA

8. If my supervisor or boss asks me to do a job, I will make sure it gets done.   ○ SD   ○ D   ○ N   ○ A   ○ SA

9. I enjoy going to parties a lot.   ○ SD   ○ D   ○ N   ○ A   ○ SA

10. Sometimes I let work tensions get the best of me.   ○ SD   ○ D   ○ N   ○ A   ○ SA

11. I would like to empower others to perform their best.   ○ SD   ○ D   ○ N   ○ A   ○ SA

12. I am considered a risk-taker, and I'm proud of it.   ○ SD   ○ D   ○ N   ○ A   ○ SA

13. Losing your temper at work is a stupid thing to do.   ○ SD   ○ D   ○ N   ○ A   ○ SA

14. I don't mind employees who take home supplies from work.   ○ SD   ○ D   ○ N   ○ A   ○ SA

15. I keep my work area as neat as possible.   ○ SD   ○ D   ○ N   ○ A   ○ SA

16. I have never felt angry at a supervisor or boss.   ○ SD   ○ D   ○ N   ○ A   ○ SA

17. I would rather do something alone than go to a party of strangers.   ○ SD   ○ D   ○ N   ○ A   ○ SA

18. I often get headaches at work due to tension.   ○ SD   ○ D   ○ N   ○ A   ○ SA

19. I like the feeling of leading a group.   ○ SD   ○ D   ○ N   ○ A   ○ SA

20. The thought of starting a business scares me a little.   ○ SD   ○ D   ○ N   ○ A   ○ SA

21. I have no friends who have difficulty in controlling their anger.   ○ SD   ○ D   ○ N   ○ A   ○ SA

22. Parents are too busy these days to have to worry about raising their children to be honest.   ○ SD   ○ D   ○ N   ○ A   ○ SA

23. I find it hard to stay focused at work sometimes.   ○ SD   ○ D   ○ N   ○ A   ○ SA

24. Nobody would ever call me the "life of the party."   ○ SD   ○ D   ○ N   ○ A   ○ SA

25. I can handle stress extremely well at work.   ○ SD   ○ D   ○ N   ○ A   ○ SA

26. Most organizations get bogged down in trivial details.   ○ SD   ○ D   ○ N   ○ A   ○ SA

27. I respect people who make decisions based on intuition.   ○ SD   ○ D   ○ N   ○ A   ○ SA

28. I used to get angry a lot at work.   ○ SD   ○ D   ○ N   ○ A   ○ SA

29. It's human nature to be at least a little dishonest.   ○ SD   ○ D   ○ N   ○ A   ○ SA

30. I can form a goal and attain it almost all the time.   ○ SD   ○ D   ○ N   ○ A   ○ SA

31. Sometimes, I've had a great time at a party of strangers.   ○ SD   ○ D   ○ N   ○ A   ○ SA

32. Almost nothing seems to make me lose my cool.   ○ SD   ○ D   ○ N   ○ A   ○ SA

33. A lot of companies fail because they are too small-minded.   ○ SD   ○ D   ○ N   ○ A   ○ SA

34. I avoid making decisions based on too little information.   ○ SD   ○ D   ○ N   ○ A   ○ SA

35. It's human nature to get angry now and then.   ○ SD   ○ D   ○ N   ○ A   ○ SA

36. Most people are honest.   ○ SD   ○ D   ○ N   ○ A   ○ SA

37. I find it hard to keep to a self-improvement program.   ○ SD   ○ D   ○ N   ○ A   ○ SA

38. I find it easy to chat with strangers on the bus or plane.   ○ SD   ○ D   ○ N   ○ A   ○ SA

39. I get tense during crises at work.   ○ SD   ○ D   ○ N   ○ A   ○ SA

40. People respond best to the fear of losing their job.   ○ SD   ○ D   ○ N   ○ A   ○ SA

41. I have never felt tired at the end of the workday.   ○ SD   ○ D   ○ N   ○ A   ○ SA

42. I have always wanted to start a successful business.   ○ SD   ○ D   ○ N   ○ A   ○ SA

43. I intensely dislike coworkers who lose their temper at times.   ○ SD   ○ D   ○ N   ○ A   ○ SA

44. I am considered very trustworthy.   ○ SD   ○ D   ○ N   ○ A   ○ SA

45. I sometimes find myself too disorganized to be truly effective at work.   ○ SD   ○ D   ○ N   ○ A   ○ SA

46. I enjoy being alone after a long workday.   ○ SD   ○ D   ○ N   ○ A   ○ SA

47. I find it hard to accept criticism sometimes.   ○ SD   ○ D   ○ N   ○ A   ○ SA

48. The future is filled with exciting possibilities.   ○ SD   ○ D   ○ N   ○ A   ○ SA

49. Risk-taking is necessary sometimes, but it should not be overdone.   ○ SD   ○ D   ○ N   ○ A   ○ SA

50. I have sometimes felt enraged at work by something stupid that a supervisor did.   ○ SD   ○ D   ○ N   ○ A   ○ SA

51. I have never made a mistake at work.   ○ SD   ○ D   ○ N   ○ A   ○ SA

52. I have never called in sick at work unless I was really ill. ⃝ SD ⃝ D ⃝ N ⃝ A ⃝ SA

53. Hard work is a key to success in life. ⃝ SD ⃝ D ⃝ N ⃝ A ⃝ SA

54. I am considered a very outgoing person. ⃝ SD ⃝ D ⃝ N ⃝ A ⃝ SA

55. I have never lost sleep worrying about losing my job. ⃝ SD ⃝ D ⃝ N ⃝ A ⃝ SA

56. To really motivate someone, find out his or her biggest goals in life. ⃝ SD ⃝ D ⃝ N ⃝ A ⃝ SA

57. I don't admire people who take risks often in business. ⃝ SD ⃝ D ⃝ N ⃝ A ⃝ SA

58. I have never felt like taking revenge against a coworker who bothered me. ⃝ SD ⃝ D ⃝ N ⃝ A ⃝ SA

59. Generally, people can be trusted. ⃝ SD ⃝ D ⃝ N ⃝ A ⃝ SA

60. I follow through on everything I ever do. ⃝ SD ⃝ D ⃝ N ⃝ A ⃝ SA

61. My job performance is usually viewed as very reliable. ⃝ SD ⃝ D ⃝ N ⃝ A ⃝ SA

62. I am a very good "mixer" at parties. ⃝ SD ⃝ D ⃝ N ⃝ A ⃝ SA

63. I am a relaxed person and can handle change well. ⃝ SD ⃝ D ⃝ N ⃝ A ⃝ SA

64. I admire a person who can get a group excited and energized. ⃝ SD ⃝ D ⃝ N ⃝ A ⃝ SA

65. We cannot avoid taking risks in life. ⃝ SD ⃝ D ⃝ N ⃝ A ⃝ SA

66. I have had a lot of irritating coworkers lately. ⃝ SD ⃝ D ⃝ N ⃝ A ⃝ SA

67. Parents should be very concerned about a teenager who has shoplifted. ⃝ SD ⃝ D ⃝ N ⃝ A ⃝ SA

68. I follow my supervisor's instructions carefully. ⃝ SD ⃝ D ⃝ N ⃝ A ⃝ SA

69. I excel at keeping a conversation going. ⃝ SD ⃝ D ⃝ N ⃝ A ⃝ SA

70. I have never snapped at a coworker because I felt tense. ⃝ SD ⃝ D ⃝ N ⃝ A ⃝ SA

71. There's something strange about people who think about the future a lot. ⃝ SD ⃝ D ⃝ N ⃝ A ⃝ SA

72. People who get bored easily are usually creative types. ⃝ SD ⃝ D ⃝ N ⃝ A ⃝ SA

73. Sometimes in my car I get mad at the stupidities of other drivers. ⃝ SD ⃝ D ⃝ N ⃝ A ⃝ SA

74. Few youngsters steal from classmates or friends. ⃝ SD ⃝ D ⃝ N ⃝ A ⃝ SA

75. The feeling of a "job well done" is overrated. ⃝ SD ⃝ D ⃝ N ⃝ A ⃝ SA

76. Most of my friends are quiet and reserved.   ○ SD   ○ D   ○ N   ○ A   ○ SA

77. I have had anxiety dreams about work.   ○ SD   ○ D   ○ N   ○ A   ○ SA

78. Life is often tedious.   ○ SD   ○ D   ○ N   ○ A   ○ SA

79. The future really makes me excited.   ○ SD   ○ D   ○ N   ○ A   ○ SA

80. People who know me well say I have a temper.   ○ SD   ○ D   ○ N   ○ A   ○ SA

81. Most people would steal a small item from a store if
they knew they would never get caught.   ○ SD   ○ D   ○ N   ○ A   ○ SA

82. People who know me never say I work too hard.   ○ SD   ○ D   ○ N   ○ A   ○ SA

83. I have sometimes worried about losing my job
because of office politics.   ○ SD   ○ D   ○ N   ○ A   ○ SA

84. "Take a chance" could not be described as my
philosophy of life.   ○ SD   ○ D   ○ N   ○ A   ○ SA

85. I get mad if I have to wait a long time in line at the
post office or the supermarket.   ○ SD   ○ D   ○ N   ○ A   ○ SA

86. High school teachers and principals should deal
strongly with students who are caught shoplifting. ○ SD   ○ D   ○ N   ○ A   ○ SA

87. Vacations are not important to me for rest and
relaxation.   ○ SD   ○ D   ○ N   ○ A   ○ SA

88. I have always planned ahead in everything.   ○ SD   ○ D   ○ N   ○ A   ○ SA

89. I like to start conversations with taxi drivers in cities
I visit.   ○ SD   ○ D   ○ N   ○ A   ○ SA

90. I enjoy having the chance to inspire people.   ○ SD   ○ D   ○ N   ○ A   ○ SA

YOUR TEST RESULTS: SAMPLE TEST #3

Scoring Method:

Strongly Disagree = 1, Disagree = 2, Neutral = 3, Agree = 4, Strongly Agree = 5

Lie Scale:

Questions 2, 16, 41, 51, 60, 88.

1. Conscientiousness

Add your scores for questions 8, 15, 30, 53, 61, 68, 87.   **TOTAL** _____

Subtract your scores for questions 23, 37, 45, 75, 82.   **TOTAL** _____

Your total score is: **TOTAL** _____

Total score = 17 or lower

You're not conscientious enough for anyone to hire you. Change your attitude, quick.

Total score = 18 to 22

Unless you get lucky, you have too little conscientiousness to be hired. Change your attitude.

Total score = 23 to 24

You probably are conscientious enough to be hired—as long as there's a tight hiring market.

Total score = 25 to 29

Your high conscientiousness will endear you to employers.

Total score = 30

You're so conscientious that your employers will hold you up as a role model.

2. *Extraversion*

Add your scores for questions 9, 31, 38, 54, 62, 69, 89.　　**TOTAL** _____

Subtract your scores for questions 1, 17, 24, 46, 76.　　**TOTAL** _____

Your total score is:　　**TOTAL** _____

Total score = 17 or lower

You're definitely an introvert and would be better off in appropriate jobs.

Total score = 18 to 22

You're on the introverted side and would be best suited for such jobs.

Total score = 23 to 24

You're probably extraverted enough to get hired for most jobs.

Total score = 25 to 29

You're definitely on the extraverted side, and employers will recognize that.

Total score = 30

You're highly extraverted and will be valued as such by employers.

3. *Integrity*

Add your scores for questions 7, 36, 44, 52, 59, 67, 74, 86.　　**TOTAL** _____

Subtract your scores for questions 14, 22, 29, 81.　　**TOTAL** _____

Your total score is:　　**TOTAL** _____

Total score = 23 or lower

> You're too low on integrity to be hired by anybody. A change of heart could help you a lot.

Total score = 24 to 27

> You're too low on integrity to attract employers. A change of heart would help.

Total Score = 28 to 31

> You've probably too little integrity to be hired by many employers. Change a few things in your outlook.

Total score = 32 to 35

> You've enough integrity to be hired by most employers.

Total score = 36

> You're a person of high integrity, or at least one who tests out that way. Employers will definitely want you.

4. *Anger*

Add your scores for questions 6, 13, 21, 43, 58.   **TOTAL** _____

Subtract your scores for questions 28, 35, 50, 66, 73, 80, 85.   **TOTAL** _____

Your total score is: **TOTAL** _____

Total score = 5 or lower

> You're a potential eruption in the workplace. Get professional help, quick.

Total score = 6 to 10

> You've got too much anger to be hired. Get professional help, the sooner the better.

Total score = 11 to 12

> You've probably too much anger to be hired. Professional help might be a good idea.

Total score = 13 to 17

> You're low enough on anger to be hired.

Total score = 18

> You're a low-anger person, and employers will value that.

5. Entrepreneurialism

Add your scores for questions 5, 12, 27, 42, 65, 72, 79.   **TOTAL** _____

Subtract your scores for questions 20, 34, 49, 57, 84.   **TOTAL** _____

Your total score is: **TOTAL** _____

Total score = 17 or lower

You definitely don't have the entrepreneurial personality. But you didn't really want to start a business, did you?

Total score = 18 to 22

You don't have the ingredients for entrepreneurship, but that shouldn't surprise you.

Total score = 23 to 24

Your entrepreneurialism may be adequate to entice employers.

Total score = 25 to 29

You have entrepreneurial talent sought by companies.

Total score = 30

You have plenty of entrepreneurial talent. Go for it.

6. Stress Tolerance

Add your scores for questions 25, 32, 55, 63, 70.   **TOTAL** _____

Subtract your scores for questions 3, 10, 18, 39, 47, 77, 83.   **TOTAL** _____

Your total score is: **TOTAL** _____

Total score = 5 or lower

Your poor ability to handle stress will turn away employers. Stress-management training would be useful.

Total score = 6 to 10

Your meager ability to handle stress won't attract employers. Stress-management training would be useful.

Total score = 11 to 12

Your ability to handle stress may be adequate to get hired.

Total score = 13 to 17

Your good ability to handle stress will be recognized by employers.

Total score = 18

Your excellent ability to handle stress will be prized by employers.

7. *Leadership*

Add your scores for questions 11, 19, 26, 33, 48, 56, 64, 90.   **TOTAL** _____

Subtract your scores for questions 4, 40, 71, 78.   **TOTAL** _____

Your total score is: **TOTAL** _____

Total score = 23 or lower

You have minimal leadership ability. Sorry, that's a fact.

Total score = 24 to 27

You don't have enough leadership ability to attract employers.

Total score = 28 to 31

You have adequate leadership ability for some employers, especially in a tight hiring market.

Total score = 32 to 35

Your leadership ability is apparent and will be recognized by employers.

Total score = 36

Your high leadership ability will be prized. Use it well.

SAMPLE PERSONALITY TEST #4

1. I am a very easy person to get to know. ○ SD ○ D ○ N ○ A ○ SA

2. People who keep the money they find in a wallet or purse on the street are not really stealing. ○ SD ○ D ○ N ○ A ○ SA

3. Most people are inspired to do their best at work. ○ SD ○ D ○ N ○ A ○ SA

4. Computer hackers are often punished too lightly. ○ SD ○ D ○ N ○ A ○ SA

5. I am very optimistic about the future. ○ SD ○ D ○ N ○ A ○ SA

6. Too many people push themselves too hard at work. ○ SD ○ D ○ N ○ A ○ SA

7. I have never talked about someone behind his or her back. ○ SD ○ D ○ N ○ A ○ SA

8. Rarely do I feel really tense at work. ○ SD ○ D ○ N ○ A ○ SA

9. People tell me it is hard to read my moods. ○ SD ○ D ○ N ○ A ○ SA

10. Employees who leave work early without permission are stealing from their company. ○ SD ○ D ○ N ○ A ○ SA

11. I believe that most people get insufficient respect at work. ○ SD ○ D ○ N ○ A ○ SA

12. It's never justifiable for a teacher to hit a student who is misbehaving. ○ SD ○ D ○ N ○ A ○ SA

13. I enjoy doing something new everyday. ○ SD ○ D ○ N ○ A ○ SA

14. People who know me say I work too hard. ○ SD ○ D ○ N ○ A ○ SA

15. I rarely feel the need to relax more at work. ○ SD ○ D ○ N ○ A ○ SA

16. I am often reserved at parties. ○ SD ○ D ○ N ○ A ○ SA

17. I don't think that anyone is totally honest. ○ SD ○ D ○ N ○ A ○ SA

18. Everybody has a big potential to be more creative at work. ○ SD ○ D ○ N ○ A ○ SA

19. Most people have fantasized about destroying equipment at work. ○ SD ○ D ○ N ○ A ○ SA

20. Without new experiences, I would find life to be tedious. ○ SD ○ D ○ N ○ A ○ SA

21. Being part of a team is basic to most jobs today. ○ SD ○ D ○ N ○ A ○ SA

22. I hardly ever worry that work will make my health suffer. ○ SD ○ D ○ N ○ A ○ SA

23. In social settings, I enjoy strolling over and introducing myself to strangers. ○ SD ○ D ○ N ○ A ○ SA

24. Employees who call in sick too often should be fired.   ○ SD   ○ D   ○ N   ○ A   ○ SA

25. The great shapers of history always looked at least five or ten years into the future.   ○ SD   ○ D   ○ N   ○ A   ○ SA

26. Most high school students have not fantasized about getting even with a teacher.   ○ SD   ○ D   ○ N   ○ A   ○ SA

27. Parents should encourage their kids to be prudent and cautious.   ○ SD   ○ D   ○ N   ○ A   ○ SA

28. I try to avoid taking on too much because I value my health.   ○ SD   ○ D   ○ N   ○ A   ○ SA

29. I rarely get upset if my work is criticized by a coworker.   ○ SD   ○ D   ○ N   ○ A   ○ SA

30. Being in a loud party usually drains me.   ○ SD   ○ D   ○ N   ○ A   ○ SA

31. I have never found loose change on the street and kept it.   ○ SD   ○ D   ○ N   ○ A   ○ SA

32. If I found a bag of money on the street, I would seriously think about keeping it.   ○ SD   ○ D   ○ N   ○ A   ○ SA

33. Some people are just born to be successful.   ○ SD   ○ D   ○ N   ○ A   ○ SA

34. I have never been bored.   ○ SD   ○ D   ○ N   ○ A   ○ SA

35. Many people lose out on opportunities because they are too cautious.   ○ SD   ○ D   ○ N   ○ A   ○ SA

36. It would be true to say that I often get angry at work.   ○ SD   ○ D   ○ N   ○ A   ○ SA

37. It's important for me to feel productive at work.   ○ SD   ○ D   ○ N   ○ A   ○ SA

38. I have felt so stressful at times that I had digestive problems.   ○ SD   ○ D   ○ N   ○ A   ○ SA

39. I'm seldom regarded as a very outgoing person.   ○ SD   ○ D   ○ N   ○ A   ○ SA

40. If I am undercharged on my restaurant bill, I always tell the waiter or waitress.   ○ SD   ○ D   ○ N   ○ A   ○ SA

41. Life is filled with endless possibilities.   ○ SD   ○ D   ○ N   ○ A   ○ SA

42. I've never felt so angry at work that I needed to step outside for a "breather."   ○ SD   ○ D   ○ N   ○ A   ○ SA

43. The thought of starting my own business scares me.   ○ SD   ○ D   ○ N   ○ A   ○ SA

44. I have almost never forgotten to show up for an appointment.   ○ SD   ○ D   ○ N   ○ A   ○ SA

45. I feel tense in thinking about my work in the future. ○ SD ○ D ○ N ○ A ○ SA

46. Most of my friends are on the shy side. ○ SD ○ D ○ N ○ A ○ SA

47. I would never knowingly buy stolen merchandise. ○ SD ○ D ○ N ○ A ○ SA

48. To be a success in life, you have got to look at least five or ten years into the future. ○ SD ○ D ○ N ○ A ○ SA

49. I believe people who say they have never lost their temper at work. ○ SD ○ D ○ N ○ A ○ SA

50. I admire people who make decisions by intuition instead of a lot of research. ○ SD ○ D ○ N ○ A ○ SA

51. I feel sorry for employees who put in long hours at work. ○ SD ○ D ○ N ○ A ○ SA

52. At a party, I have never said the wrong thing to anybody. ○ SD ○ D ○ N ○ A ○ SA

53. I have often had anxiety dreams about work. ○ SD ○ D ○ N ○ A ○ SA

54. I easily make "small talk" when sitting next to a stranger on the train or plane. ○ SD ○ D ○ N ○ A ○ SA

55. If an employee receives too much money on a paycheck, it's not his or her responsibility to report it. ○ SD ○ D ○ N ○ A ○ SA

56. There's something abnormal about someone who thinks a lot about the future. ○ SD ○ D ○ N ○ A ○ SA

57. I would not hire someone who said, "My philosophy is: don't get angry. Get even." ○ SD ○ D ○ N ○ A ○ SA

58. Most of my friends are risk-takers. ○ SD ○ D ○ N ○ A ○ SA

59. Employees should be expected to finish a job, no matter how long it takes. ○ SD ○ D ○ N ○ A ○ SA

60. I would have to admit that work is the most stressful thing in my life. ○ SD ○ D ○ N ○ A ○ SA

61. I can't recall the last time I told a joke at a party. ○ SD ○ D ○ N ○ A ○ SA

62. I am known to have a terrific personality. ○ SD ○ D ○ N ○ A ○ SA

63. I am outraged by parents who don't care if their children steal at school. ○ SD ○ D ○ N ○ A ○ SA

64. To inspire employees, you must offer them a big goal they can endorse. ○ SD ○ D ○ N ○ A ○ SA

65. I have sometimes really felt like hitting a supervisor. ○ SD ○ D ○ N ○ A ○ SA

66. I have taken risks that really paid off in my life. ○ SD ○ D ○ N ○ A ○ SA

67. People who know me consider me a "team
    player."　　　　　　　　　○ SD　○ D　○ N　○ A　○ SA

68. I just can't seem to unwind easily after work.　○ SD　○ D　○ N　○ A　○ SA

69. In conversations, I usually let the other person do the
    talking.　　　　　　　　　○ SD　○ D　○ N　○ A　○ SA

70. My friends consider me extremely honest when it
    comes to money.　　　　○ SD　○ D　○ N　○ A　○ SA

71. Every employee should be treated with dignity.　○ SD　○ D　○ N　○ A　○ SA

72. People who rely a lot on intuition are going to fail in
    business.　　　　　　　　○ SD　○ D　○ N　○ A　○ SA

73. I have found it hard to contain my anger sometimes.　○ SD　○ D　○ N　○ A　○ SA

74. Vacations are important to give people a balance in
    their lives.　　　　　　　○ SD　○ D　○ N　○ A　○ SA

75. I have never missed a day due to illness.　○ SD　○ D　○ N　○ A　○ SA

76. On weekends, I find myself still feeling stress
    from work.　　　　　　　○ SD　○ D　○ N　○ A　○ SA

77. I can find something to chat about with nearly
    everyone.　　　　　　　　○ SD　○ D　○ N　○ A　○ SA

78. Employees who take home minor supplies are not
    really stealing.　　　　　○ SD　○ D　○ N　○ A　○ SA

79. Employees who dislike their work are rarely highly
    productive.　　　　　　　○ SD　○ D　○ N　○ A　○ SA

80. I have a few friends who get angry too easily.　○ SD　○ D　○ N　○ A　○ SA

81. Teachers should teach students to make decisions
    without a lot of research.　○ SD　○ D　○ N　○ A　○ SA

82. I try to keep lunch breaks short in order to accomplish
    more on the job.　　　　○ SD　○ D　○ N　○ A　○ SA

83. I know my health has gotten worse lately due to
    stress.　　　　　　　　　○ SD　○ D　○ N　○ A　○ SA

84. I almost never avoid meeting new groups of people.　○ SD　○ D　○ N　○ A　○ SA

85. If someone is undercharged at a convenience store, he
    or she should definitely tell the clerk.　○ SD　○ D　○ N　○ A　○ SA

86. Nothing motivates employees more than fear of
    losing their jobs.　　　　○ SD　○ D　○ N　○ A　○ SA

87. Employees who destroy equipment at work never
    have a good reason for doing so.　○ SD　○ D　○ N　○ A　○ SA

88. The most successful people are those who finish a job
    no matter how long it takes.   ○ SD   ○ D   ○ N   ○ A   ○ SA

89. I like doing familiar things.   ○ SD   ○ D   ○ N   ○ A   ○ SA

90. I never worry about whether I can handle all my work
    responsibilities.   ○ SD   ○ D   ○ N   ○ A   ○ SA

YOUR TEST RESULTS: PERSONALITY TEST #4

Scoring Method:

Strongly Disagree = 1, Disagree = 2, Neutral = 3, Agree = 4, Strongly Agree = 5

Lie Scale:

Add your scores for questions 7, 31, 34, 52, 62, 75.   **TOTAL** _____

> If your total score = 30, the alarm bell is screeching.
> If your total score is 24 to 29, the alarm is loud.
> If your total score is 19 to 23, the alarm is soft but clear.
> If your total score is 18 or lower, the alarm is silent.

1. Conscientiousness

Add your scores for questions 14, 21, 37, 44, 59, 67,
82, 88.   **TOTAL** _____

Subtract your scores for questions 6, 28, 51, 74.   **TOTAL** _____

Your total score is: **TOTAL** _____

> Total score = 23 or lower
>> You're not conscientious enough for anyone to hire you. Change your attitude, quick.

> Total score = 24 to 27
>> Unless you get lucky, you have too little conscientiousness to be hired. Change your attitude.

> Total score = 28 to 31
>> You probably are conscientious enough to be hired—as long as there's a tight hiring market.

> Total score = 32 to 35
>> Your high conscientiousness will endear you to your employers.

> Total score = 36
>> You're so conscientious that your employers will hold you up as a role model.

2. *Extraversion*

Add your scores for questions 1, 23, 54, 77, 84.   **TOTAL** _____

Subtract your scores for questions 9, 16, 30, 39, 46, 61, 69.   **TOTAL** _____

Your total score is: **TOTAL** _____

Total score = 5 or lower

You're definitely an introvert and would be better off in appropriate jobs.

Total score = 6 to 10

You're on the introverted side and would be best suited for such jobs.

Total score = 11 to 12

You're probably extraverted enough to get hired for most jobs.

Total score = 13 to 17

You're definitely on the extraverted side, and employers will recognize that.

Total score = 18

You're highly extraverted and will be valued as such by employers.

3. *Integrity*

Add your scores for questions 10, 24, 40, 47, 63, 70, 85.   **TOTAL** _____

Subtract your scores for questions 2, 17, 32, 55, 78.   **TOTAL** _____

Your total score is: **TOTAL** _____

Total score = 17 or lower

You're too low on integrity to be hired by anybody. A change of heart could help you a lot.

Total score = 18 to 22

You're too low on integrity to attract employers. A change of heart would help.

Total score = 23 to 24

You've probably too little integrity to be hired by many employers. Change a few things in your outlook.

Total score = 25 to 29

You've enough integrity to be hired by most employers.

Total score = 30

You're a person of high integrity, or at least one who tests out that way. Employers will definitely want you.

4. *Anger*

Add your scores for questions 4, 12, 26, 42, 49, 57, 87. **TOTAL** _____

Subtract your scores for questions 19, 36, 65, 73, 80. **TOTAL** _____

Your total score is: **TOTAL** _____

Total score = 17 or lower

You're a potential eruption in the workplace. Get professional help, quick.

Total score = 18 to 22

You've got too much anger to be hired. Get professional help, the sooner the better.

Total score = 23 to 24

You've probably too much anger to be hired. Professional help might be a good idea.

Total score = 25 to 29

You're low enough on anger to be hired.

Total score = 30

You're a low-anger person, and employers will value that.

5. *Entrepreneurialism*

Add your scores for questions 5, 13, 20, 35, 50, 58, 66, 81. **TOTAL** _____

Subtract your scores for questions 27, 43, 72, 89. **TOTAL** _____

Your total score is: **TOTAL** _____

Total score = 23 or lower

You definitely don't have the entrepreneurial personality. But you didn't really want to start a business, did you?

Total score = 24 to 27

You don't have the ingredients for entrepreneurship, but that shouldn't surprise you.

Total score = 28 to 31

Your entrepreneurialism may be adequate to entice employers.

Total score = 32 to 35

You have entrepreneurial talent sought by employers.

Total score = 36

You have plenty of entrepreneurial talent. Go for it.

6. Stress Tolerance

Add your scores for questions 8, 15, 22, 29, 90.   **TOTAL** _____

Subtract your scores for questions 38, 45, 53, 60, 68, 76, 83.   **TOTAL** _____

Your total score is: **TOTAL** _____

Total score = 5 or lower

Your poor ability to handle stress will turn away employers. Stress-management training would be useful.

Total score = 6 to 10

Your meager ability to handle stress won't attract employers. Stress-management training would be useful.

Total score = 11 to 12

Your ability to handle stress may be adequate to get hired.

Total score = 13 to 17

Your good ability to handle stress will be recognized by employers.

Total score = 18

Your excellent ability to handle stress will be prized by employers.

7. Leadership

Add your scores for questions 11, 18, 25, 41, 48, 64, 71, 79.   **TOTAL** _____

Subtract your scores for questions 3, 33, 56, 86.   **TOTAL** _____

Your total score is: **TOTAL** _____

Total score = 23 or lower

You have minimal leadership ability. Sorry, that's a fact.

Total score = 24 to 27

You don't have enough leadership ability to attract employers.

Total score = 28 to 31

You have adequate leadership ability for some employers, especially in a tight hiring market.

Total score = 32 to 35

Your leadership ability is apparent and will be recognized by employers.

Total score = 36

Your high leadership ability will be prized. Use it well.

SAMPLE PERSONALITY TEST #5

1. I feel happiest in doing familiar things. ○ SD ○ D ○ N ○ A ○ SA

2. People who don't work hard for their employer should not keep their jobs. ○ SD ○ D ○ N ○ A ○ SA

3. I seem to handle stress better than most of my coworkers. ○ SD ○ D ○ N ○ A ○ SA

4. I find making "small talk" with strangers to be unpleasant. ○ SD ○ D ○ N ○ A ○ SA

5. I would like to lead an organization. ○ SD ○ D ○ N ○ A ○ SA

6. I have never met a totally honest person. ○ SD ○ D ○ N ○ A ○ SA

7. I have never felt enraged at work. ○ SD ○ D ○ N ○ A ○ SA

8. I would not be considered a risk-taker by my friends. ○ SD ○ D ○ N ○ A ○ SA

9. My friends would consider me very hardworking. ○ SD ○ D ○ N ○ A ○ SA

10. I have almost never felt like crying due to work tension. ○ SD ○ D ○ N ○ A ○ SA

11. I prefer to work alone rather than in a group. ○ SD ○ D ○ N ○ A ○ SA

12. My friends consider me a "born leader." ○ SD ○ D ○ N ○ A ○ SA

13. It's human nature to steal a little at times. ○ SD ○ D ○ N ○ A ○ SA

14. If someone criticizes my work, I almost never lose my temper. ○ SD ○ D ○ N ○ A ○ SA

15. Children should be taught to make decisions only after they have all the information. ○ SD ○ D ○ N ○ A ○ SA

16. If I start a project, you can be sure I will finish it. ○ SD ○ D ○ N ○ A ○ SA

17. I rarely feel drained after a long workday. ○ SD ○ D ○ N ○ A ○ SA

18. I like to be at loud parties. ○ SD ○ D ○ N ○ A ○ SA

19. Most people are not sufficiently motivated at work. ○ SD ○ D ○ N ○ A ○ SA

20. I have never been accused of taking something that belonged to others. ○ SD ○ D ○ N ○ A ○ SA

21. Most of my friends would say I get easily angered. ○ SD ○ D ○ N ○ A ○ SA

22. The thought of starting my own business excites me. ○ SD ○ D ○ N ○ A ○ SA

23. I would never hire someone who seemed to be a "slacker" in his or her work attitude. ○ SD ○ D ○ N ○ A ○ SA

24. I have overeaten sometimes due to work stress. ○ SD ○ D ○ N ○ A ○ SA

25. I feel energized when part of a large crowd. ○ SD ○ D ○ N ○ A ○ SA

26. I like to think about the future.   O SD   O D   O N   O A   O SA

27. Honesty about money is central to my value system.   O SD   O D   O N   O A   O SA

28. Controlling my temper has never been a problem
    for me.   O SD   O D   O N   O A   O SA

29. The most successful people in business take risks
    often.   O SD   O D   O N   O A   O SA

30. The path to success lies in putting in long hours at
    work.   O SD   O D   O N   O A   O SA

31. I sometimes have trouble sleeping at night due to
    thinking about work.   O SD   O D   O N   O A   O SA

32. In most party situations, I just "go with the flow" and
    have fun.   O SD   O D   O N   O A   O SA

33. The best way to motivate an employee is to threaten
    job termination.   O SD   O D   O N   O A   O SA

34. I have never been tempted to shoplift.   O SD   O D   O N   O A   O SA

35. If teachers were allowed to hit students who
    misbehave, our schools would be a better place.   O SD   O D   O N   O A   O SA

36. I trust my intuition a great deal.   O SD   O D   O N   O A   O SA

37. I think a lot about nice vacations I'd like to take. O SD   O D   O N   O A   O SA

38. Sometimes I have felt too stressed after work to eat
    dinner.   O SD   O D   O N   O A   O SA

39. I like to be the center of attention at a party.   O SD   O D   O N   O A   O SA

40. People achieve more when they can aim for a big
    goal.   O SD   O D   O N   O A   O SA

41. I think most teenagers have thought about
    shoplifting.   O SD   O D   O N   O A   O SA

42. An employee who loses his or her temper frequently
    should be fired.   O SD   O D   O N   O A   O SA

43. I have often been praised for my excellent intuition. O SD   O D   O N   O A   O SA

44. I have never jaywalked.   O SD   O D   O N   O A   O SA

45. I have never felt lonely.   O SD   O D   O N   O A   O SA

46. I find it hard to "party" with people I don't know
    well.   O SD   O D   O N   O A   O SA

47. Most people have a huge unused potential.   O SD   O D   O N   O A   O SA

48. Parents who let their children steal from classmates
    disgust me.   O SD   O D   O N   O A   O SA

49. I sometimes get angry when stuck on the road behind a bad driver.   ○ SD ○ D ○ N ○ A ○ SA

50. I like to make decisions based on my intuition.   ○ SD ○ D ○ N ○ A ○ SA

51. I sometimes have difficulty finishing what I start.   ○ SD ○ D ○ N ○ A ○ SA

52. I often feel sad.   ○ SD ○ D ○ N ○ A ○ SA

53. The thought of making sales calls to strangers scares me a little.   ○ SD ○ D ○ N ○ A ○ SA

54. I get excited in thinking about big projects I'd like to accomplish.   ○ SD ○ D ○ N ○ A ○ SA

55. Nobody I know has ever shoplifted.   ○ SD ○ D ○ N ○ A ○ SA

56. I get irritated if I wait too long in a line at the supermarket.   ○ SD ○ D ○ N ○ A ○ SA

57. To make a decision without having all the facts usually leads to failure.   ○ SD ○ D ○ N ○ A ○ SA

58. Self-improvement programs don't seem to work for me.   ○ SD ○ D ○ N ○ A ○ SA

59. At times, I have felt like quitting a job due to its stress.   ○ SD ○ D ○ N ○ A ○ SA

60. I would never enjoy making frequent sales calls to strangers.   ○ SD ○ D ○ N ○ A ○ SA

61. People who think about the future a lot are a bit strange.   ○ SD ○ D ○ N ○ A ○ SA

62. Schools should get tougher on students who take things from classmates.   ○ SD ○ D ○ N ○ A ○ SA

63. An employee who sends an angry e-mail to a coworker should definitely be reprimanded by his or her supervisor.   ○ SD ○ D ○ N ○ A ○ SA

64. I would never want the stress of starting my own business.   ○ SD ○ D ○ N ○ A ○ SA

65. I keep my work area tidy and organized.   ○ SD ○ D ○ N ○ A ○ SA

66. I don't handle myself well in emergencies.   ○ SD ○ D ○ N ○ A ○ SA

67. Most of my friends are on the "loud" side.   ○ SD ○ D ○ N ○ A ○ SA

68. I have never had a headache.   ○ SD ○ D ○ N ○ A ○ SA

69. To be successful, it's important to have big goals in life.   ○ SD ○ D ○ N ○ A ○ SA

70. Our society's laws against shoplifting are not tough enough.   ○ SD ○ D ○ N ○ A ○ SA

71. "Road rage" is a serious problem today in our country.   ○ SD ○ D ○ N ○ A ○ SA

72. The most successful people in history avoided risks in their lives. ○ SD ○ D ○ N ○ A ○ SA

73. My friends would not call me a highly organized person. ○ SD ○ D ○ N ○ A ○ SA

74. I seem to worry more than most people my age. ○ SD ○ D ○ N ○ A ○ SA

75. I usually let the other person talk when in a conversation. ○ SD ○ D ○ N ○ A ○ SA

76. I have been praised for my ability to motivate people around me. ○ SD ○ D ○ N ○ A ○ SA

77. I have fantasized about getting away with a big robbery. ○ SD ○ D ○ N ○ A ○ SA

78. An employee who sends a coworker a threatening e-mail should be fired immediately. ○ SD ○ D ○ N ○ A ○ SA

79. I have many new ideas that I'd like to try out. ○ SD ○ D ○ N ○ A ○ SA

80. I have never lost a friend. ○ SD ○ D ○ N ○ A ○ SA

81. I pay attention to my goals nearly everyday. ○ SD ○ D ○ N ○ A ○ SA

82. My health has never suffered because of work stress. ○ SD ○ D ○ N ○ A ○ SA

83. I am known to have no faults. ○ SD ○ D ○ N ○ A ○ SA

84. At meetings, people often look to me for direction. ○ SD ○ D ○ N ○ A ○ SA

85. My friends would say I seldom get angry. ○ SD ○ D ○ N ○ A ○ SA

86. It's really not stealing if an employee sometimes takes home supplies. ○ SD ○ D ○ N ○ A ○ SA

87. I have never been late for an appointment. ○ SD ○ D ○ N ○ A ○ SA

88. Sometimes I admire computer hackers who can damage company property and not be caught. ○ SD ○ D ○ N ○ A ○ SA

89. I sometimes give up when a task gets me frustrated. ○ SD ○ D ○ N ○ A ○ SA

90. I hardly ever feel tension at work. ○ SD ○ D ○ N ○ A ○ SA

YOUR TEST RESULTS: PERSONALITY TEST #5

Scoring Method:

Strongly Disagree = 1, Disagree = 2, Neutral = 3, Agree = 4, Strongly Agree = 5

Lie Scale:

Add your scores for questions 44, 45, 68, 80, 83, 87. **TOTAL** _____

If your total score = 30, the alarm bell is screeching.

If your total score is 24 to 29, the alarm is loud.

If your total score is 19 to 23, the alarm is soft but clear.

If your total score is 18 or lower, the alarm is silent.

1. *Conscientiousness*

Add your scores for questions 2, 9, 16, 23, 30, 65, 81.   **TOTAL** _____

Subtract your scores for questions 37, 51, 58, 73, 89.   **TOTAL** _____

Your total score: **TOTAL** _____

Total score = 17 or lower

> You're not conscientious enough for anyone to hire you. Change your attitude, quick.

Total score = 18 to 22

> Unless you get lucky, you have too little conscientiousness to be hired. Change your attitude.

Total score = 23 to 24

> You probably are conscientious enough to be hired—as long as there's a tight hiring market.

Total score = 25 to 29

> Your high conscientiousness will endear you to employers.

Total score = 30

> You're so conscientious that your employers will hold you up as a role model.

2. *Extraversion*

Add your scores for questions 18, 25, 32, 39, 67.   **TOTAL** _____

Subtract your scores for questions 4, 11, 46, 53, 60, 75, 85.   **TOTAL** _____

Your total score: **TOTAL** _____

Total score = 5 or lower

> You're definitely an introvert and would be better off in appropriate jobs.

Total score = 6 to 10

> You're on the introverted side and would be best suited for such jobs.

Total score = 11 to 12

> You're probably extraverted enough to get hired for most jobs.

Total score = 13 to 17

> You're definitely on the extraverted side, and employers will recognize that.

Total score = 18

You're highly extraverted and will be valued as such by employers.

3. *Integrity*

Add your scores for questions 20, 27, 34, 48, 55, 62, 70.   **TOTAL** _____

Subtract your scores for questions 6, 13, 41, 77, 86.   **TOTAL** _____

Your total score: **TOTAL** _____

Total score = 17 or lower

You're too low on integrity to be hired by anybody. A change of heart could help you a lot.

Total score = 18 to 22

You're too low on integrity to attract employers. A change of heart would help.

Total score = 23 to 24

You've probably too little integrity to be hired by many employers. Change a few things in your outlook.

Total score = 25 to 29

You've enough integrity to be hired by most employers.

Total score = 30

You're a person of high integrity, or at least one who tests out that way. Employers will definitely want you.

4. *Anger*

Add your scores for questions 7, 14, 28, 42, 63, 71, 78.   **TOTAL** _____

Subtract your scores for questions 21, 35, 49, 56, 88.   **TOTAL** _____

Your total score: **TOTAL** _____

Total score = 17 or lower

You're a potential eruption in the workplace. Get professional help, quick.

Total score = 18 to 22

You've got too much anger to be hired. Get professional help, the sooner the better.

Total score = 23 to 24

You've probably too much anger to be hired. Professional help might be a good idea.

Total score = 25 to 29

You're low enough on anger to be hired.

Total score = 30

You're a low-anger person, and employers will value that.

5. *Entrepreneurialism*

Add your scores for questions 22, 29, 36, 43, 50, 79.   **TOTAL** _____

Subtract your scores for questions 1, 8, 15, 57, 64, 72.   **TOTAL** _____

Your total score: **TOTAL** _____

Total score = 11 or lower

You definitely don't have the entrepreneurial personality. But you didn't really want to start a business, did you?

Total score = 12 to 17

You don't have the ingredients for entrepreneurship, but that shouldn't surprise you.

Total score = 18 to 21

Your entrepreneurialism may be adequate to entice employers.

Total score = 22 to 23

You have entrepreneurial talent sought by employers.

Total score = 24

You have plenty of entrepreneurial talent. Go for it.

6. *Stress Tolerance*

Add your scores for questions 3, 10, 17, 82, 90.   **TOTAL** _____

Subtract your scores for questions 24, 31, 38, 52, 59, 66, 74.   **TOTAL** _____

Your total score: **TOTAL** _____

Total score = 5 or lower

Your poor ability to handle stress will turn away employers. Stress-management training would be useful.

Total score = 6 to 10

Your meager ability to handle stress won't attract employers. Stress-management training would be useful.

Total score = 11 to 12

Your ability to handle stress may be adequate to get hired.

Total score = 13 to 17

> Your good ability to handle stress will be recognized by employers.

Total score = 18

> Your excellent ability to handle stress will be prized by employers.

7. *Leadership*

Add your scores for questions 5, 12, 19, 26, 40, 47, 54, 69, 76, 84.   **TOTAL** _____

Subtract your scores for questions 33, 61.   **TOTAL** _____

Your total score: **TOTAL** _____

Total score = 35 or lower

> You have minimal leadership ability. Sorry, that's a fact.

Total score = 36 to 37

> You don't have enough leadership ability to attract employers.

Total score = 38 to 45

> You have adequate leadership ability for some employers, especially in a tight hiring market.

Total score = 46 to 47

> Your leadership ability is apparent and will be recognized by employers.

Total score = 48

> Your high leadership ability will be prized. Use it well.

SAMPLE PERSONALITY TEST #6

1. I am one of the most hardworking persons I know.   ○ SD   ○ D   ○ N   ○ A   ○ SA

2. My feelings do not get hurt easily.   ○ SD   ○ D   ○ N   ○ A   ○ SA

3. I am considered the "life of the party" by my friends.   ○ SD   ○ D   ○ N   ○ A   ○ SA

4. I take pride in almost never losing my temper.   ○ SD   ○ D   ○ N   ○ A   ○ SA

5. I have almost never been tempted to steal.   ○ SD   ○ D   ○ N   ○ A   ○ SA

6. I would not like to lead an organization.   ○ SD   ○ D   ○ N   ○ A   ○ SA

7. I can't imagine wanting to start my own business.   ○ SD   ○ D   ○ N   ○ A   ○ SA

8. I sometimes give up if I can't solve a work problem.   ○ SD   ○ D   ○ N   ○ A   ○ SA

9. I handle criticism better than most people I know.   ○ SD   ○ D   ○ N   ○ A   ○ SA

10. I enjoy making "small talk" with strangers in line at the post office.   ○ SD   ○ D   ○ N   ○ A   ○ SA

11. I get easily insulted.   ○ SD   ○ D   ○ N   ○ A   ○ SA

12. On one occasion, I shoplifted as a teenager.   ○ SD   ○ D   ○ N   ○ A   ○ SA

13. The thought of motivating a group of people excites me.   ○ SD   ○ D   ○ N   ○ A   ○ SA

14. People who start their own business work much too hard.   ○ SD   ○ D   ○ N   ○ A   ○ SA

15. I am willing to work evenings if the job requires it.   ○ SD   ○ D   ○ N   ○ A   ○ SA

16. My friends do not consider me overly sensitive.   ○ SD   ○ D   ○ N   ○ A   ○ SA

17. I avoid loud parties.   ○ SD   ○ D   ○ N   ○ A   ○ SA

18. Angry employees should not be tolerated by their companies.   ○ SD   ○ D   ○ N   ○ A   ○ SA

19. I don't know anyone personally who shoplifted as a teenager.   ○ SD   ○ D   ○ N   ○ A   ○ SA

20. Successful people often think five or ten years into the future.   ○ SD   ○ D   ○ N   ○ A   ○ SA

21. Most people who take risks in business end up as failures.   ○ SD   ○ D   ○ N   ○ A   ○ SA

22. I am very punctual about appointments.   ○ SD   ○ D   ○ N   ○ A   ○ SA

23. I sometimes lose sleep worrying about work.   ○ SD   ○ D   ○ N   ○ A   ○ SA

24. After a long workday, I prefer to be by myself.   ⃝ SD ⃝ D ⃝ N ⃝ A ⃝ SA

25. There is no excuse for losing one's temper at work. ⃝ SD ⃝ D ⃝ N ⃝ A ⃝ SA

26. Parents should make honesty a top priority for their children's values.   ⃝ SD ⃝ D ⃝ N ⃝ A ⃝ SA

27. Most employees are not motivated enough to achieve.   ⃝ SD ⃝ D ⃝ N ⃝ A ⃝ SA

28. Risk-taking is something that's hard for me to do.   ⃝ SD ⃝ D ⃝ N ⃝ A ⃝ SA

29. I am considered a reliable person if a job needs to be done on time.   ⃝ SD ⃝ D ⃝ N ⃝ A ⃝ SA

30. I know my health has suffered because of work tension.   ⃝ SD ⃝ D ⃝ N ⃝ A ⃝ SA

31. I don't like to be the center of attention at a party.   ⃝ SD ⃝ D ⃝ N ⃝ A ⃝ SA

32. It's human nature to get angry at others now and then.   ⃝ SD ⃝ D ⃝ N ⃝ A ⃝ SA

33. Our schools don't stress the importance of honesty enough.   ⃝ SD ⃝ D ⃝ N ⃝ A ⃝ SA

34. Too many companies get bogged down in day-to-day details.   ⃝ SD ⃝ D ⃝ N ⃝ A ⃝ SA

35. I almost never make a decision based on my intuition.   ⃝ SD ⃝ D ⃝ N ⃝ A ⃝ SA

36. I admire people who work very hard for their companies.   ⃝ SD ⃝ D ⃝ N ⃝ A ⃝ SA

37. I would have to agree that work is highly stressful for me.   ⃝ SD ⃝ D ⃝ N ⃝ A ⃝ SA

38. Being part of a big crowd energizes me.   ⃝ SD ⃝ D ⃝ N ⃝ A ⃝ SA

39. The topic of workplace violence is overexaggerated by the newspapers.   ⃝ SD ⃝ D ⃝ N ⃝ A ⃝ SA

40. I am known to be a very honest person.   ⃝ SD ⃝ D ⃝ N ⃝ A ⃝ SA

41. The big picture is more important than little details for true success.   ⃝ SD ⃝ D ⃝ N ⃝ A ⃝ SA

42. Students should learn how to make decisions without having all the facts.   ⃝ SD ⃝ D ⃝ N ⃝ A ⃝ SA

43. I do not fantasize much about taking a nice, long vacation.   ⃝ SD ⃝ D ⃝ N ⃝ A ⃝ SA

44. I am admired by everyone who has ever met me.   ○ SD   ○ D   ○ N   ○ A   ○ SA

45. I handle emergencies very well.   ○ SD   ○ D   ○ N   ○ A   ○ SA

46. I usually enjoy a quiet get-together rather than being in a loud group.   ○ SD   ○ D   ○ N   ○ A   ○ SA

47. I would not hire someone who admitted to having a problem controlling his or her anger.   ○ SD   ○ D   ○ N   ○ A   ○ SA

48. An employee who takes home supplies sometimes should be reprimanded, and then fired if it continues.   ○ SD   ○ D   ○ N   ○ A   ○ SA

49. I like to think about the future and its possibilities.   ○ SD   ○ D   ○ N   ○ A   ○ SA

50. I admire people who take risks frequently in business.   ○ SD   ○ D   ○ N   ○ A   ○ SA

51. I must admit to being disorganized sometimes at work.   ○ SD   ○ D   ○ N   ○ A   ○ SA

52. I have lost weight sometimes due to work stress.   ○ SD   ○ D   ○ N   ○ A   ○ SA

53. I often tell jokes at parties.   ○ SD   ○ D   ○ N   ○ A   ○ SA

54. We all lose our temper from time to time.   ○ SD   ○ D   ○ N   ○ A   ○ SA

55. People are basically honest.   ○ SD   ○ D   ○ N   ○ A   ○ SA

56. Employees who worry about job security are not likely to be productive.   ○ SD   ○ D   ○ N   ○ A   ○ SA

57. I have a lot of new ideas.   ○ SD   ○ D   ○ N   ○ A   ○ SA

58. I have never felt sad.   ○ SD   ○ D   ○ N   ○ A   ○ SA

59. Being successful on the job is a key value for me.   ○ SD   ○ D   ○ N   ○ A   ○ SA

60. If I have an argument at work, I usually keep thinking about it that evening.   ○ SD   ○ D   ○ N   ○ A   ○ SA

61. My friends consider me a basically shy person.   ○ SD   ○ D   ○ N   ○ A   ○ SA

62. I often get irritated by the stupid mistakes of coworkers.   ○ SD   ○ D   ○ N   ○ A   ○ SA

63. It's a form of stealing to call in sick at work if you just want a day to relax.   ○ SD   ○ D   ○ N   ○ A   ○ SA

64. If you can give someone a big goal to strive for, he or she will become energized.   ○ SD   ○ D   ○ N   ○ A   ○ SA

65. I would have to admit that I get bored easily.   ○ SD   ○ D   ○ N   ○ A   ○ SA

66. When I give my word that I will do something, you can count on it.   ○ SD   ○ D   ○ N   ○ A   ○ SA

67. I let little things bother me on the job.
    ○ SD ○ D ○ N ○ A ○ SA

68. I'm able to talk with strangers about almost anything.
    ○ SD ○ D ○ N ○ A ○ SA

69. I sometimes get angry when driving in rush-hour traffic.
    ○ SD ○ D ○ N ○ A ○ SA

70. Leaving work early without permission isn't really stealing from anyone.
    ○ SD ○ D ○ N ○ A ○ SA

71. I have rarely been interested in becoming head of a club or after-school activity.
    ○ SD ○ D ○ N ○ A ○ SA

72. I have never deceived anyone.
    ○ SD ○ D ○ N ○ A ○ SA

73. I have always been polite to everyone.
    ○ SD ○ D ○ N ○ A ○ SA

74. Many creative people need constant new activities.
    ○ SD ○ D ○ N ○ A ○ SA

75. I have never been late for an appointment.
    ○ SD ○ D ○ N ○ A ○ SA

76. I am not especially tidy in my workspace.
    ○ SD ○ D ○ N ○ A ○ SA

77. I seem to worry more than most people I know.
    ○ SD ○ D ○ N ○ A ○ SA

78. It's hard for people to know what I am feeling.
    ○ SD ○ D ○ N ○ A ○ SA

79. I rarely get impatient when waiting in a line at the supermarket.
    ○ SD ○ D ○ N ○ A ○ SA

80. If I saw a coworker leave work early without permission, I would tell my supervisor.
    ○ SD ○ D ○ N ○ A ○ SA

81. Most employees aren't given enough respect for their work.
    ○ SD ○ D ○ N ○ A ○ SA

82. I feel it's important to do a job thoroughly, or not at all.
    ○ SD ○ D ○ N ○ A ○ SA

83. I have seldom thought about quitting a job due to its stress.
    ○ SD ○ D ○ N ○ A ○ SA

84. My moods are obvious to most people who know me.
    ○ SD ○ D ○ N ○ A ○ SA

85. I would fire an employee who often yelled at others.
    ○ SD ○ D ○ N ○ A ○ SA

86. I never missed a schoolday because of illness.
    ○ SD ○ D ○ N ○ A ○ SA

87. It's human nature to be tempted to steal at least occasionally.
    ○ SD ○ D ○ N ○ A ○ SA

88. Every person should be treated with dignity. ◯ SD ◯ D ◯ N ◯ A ◯ SA

89. My friends would say I prefer familiar activities to new ones. ◯ SD ◯ D ◯ N ◯ A ◯ SA

90. I like to visit new places frequently. ◯ SD ◯ D ◯ N ◯ A ◯ SA

YOUR TEST RESULTS: PERSONALITY TEST #6

Scoring Method:

Strongly Disagree = 1, Disagree = 2, Neutral = 3, Agree = 4, Strongly Agree = 5

Lie Scale:

Add your scores for questions 44, 58, 72, 73, 75, 86.

If your total score = 30, the alarm bell is screeching.
If your total score is 24 to 29, the alarm is loud.
If your total score is 19 to 23, the alarm is soft but clear.
If your total score is 18 or lower, the alarm is silent.

1. Conscientiousness

Add your scores for questions 1, 15, 22, 29, 36, 43, 59, 66, 82. TOTAL _____

Subtract your scores for questions 8, 51, 76. TOTAL _____

Your total score is: TOTAL _____

Total score = 29 or lower

You're not conscientious enough for anyone to hire you. Change your attitude, quick.

Total score = 30 to 32

Unless you get lucky, you have too little conscientiousness to be hired. Change your attitude.

Total score = 33 to 35

You probably are conscientious enough to be hired—as long as there's a tight hiring market.

Total score = 36 to 41

Your high conscientiousness will endear you to employers.

Total score = 42

> You're so conscientious that your employers will hold you up as a role model.

2. *Extraversion*

Add your scores for questions 3, 10, 38, 53, 68, 84.   **TOTAL** _____

Subtract your scores for questions 17, 24, 31, 46, 61, 78.   **TOTAL** _____

Your total score is: **TOTAL** _____

Total score = 11 or lower

> You're definitely an introvert and would be better off in appropriate jobs.

Total score = 12 to 17

> You're on the introverted side and would be best suited for such jobs.

Total score = 18 to 21

> You're probably extraverted enough to get hired for most jobs.

Total score = 22 to 23

> You're definitely on the extraverted side, and employers will recognize that.

Total score = 24

> You're highly extraverted and will be valued as such by employers.

3. *Integrity*

Add your scores for questions 5, 19, 26, 33, 40, 48, 55, 63, 80.   **TOTAL** _____

Subtract your scores for questions 12, 70, 87.   **TOTAL** _____

Your total score is: **TOTAL** _____

Total score = 29 or lower

> You're too low on integrity to be hired by anybody. A change of heart could help you a lot.

Total score = 30 to 32

> You're too low on integrity to attract employers. A change of heart would help.

Total score = 33 to 35

> You've probably too little integrity to be hired by many employers. Change a few things in your outlook.

Total score = 36 to 41

You've enough integrity to be hired by most employers.

Total score = 42

You're a person of high integrity, or at least one who tests out that way. Employers will definitely want you.

4. *Anger*

Add your scores for questions 4, 18, 25, 47, 79, 85.　　**TOTAL** _____

Subtract your scores for questions 11, 32, 39, 54, 62, 69.　**TOTAL** _____

Your total score is:　　**TOTAL** _____

Total score = 11 or lower

You're a potential eruption in the workplace. Get professional help, quick.

Total score = 12 to 17

You've got too much anger to be hired. Get professional help, the sooner the better.

Total score = 18 to 21

You've probably too much anger to be hired. Professional help might be a good idea.

Total score = 22 to 23

You're low enough on anger to be hired.

Total score = 24

You're a low-anger person, and employers will value that.

5. *Entrepreneurialism*

Add your scores for questions 42, 50, 57, 65, 74, 89, 90.　**TOTAL** _____

Subtract your scores for questions 7, 14, 21, 28, 35.　　**TOTAL** _____

Your total score:　　**TOTAL** _____

Total score = 17 or lower

You definitely don't have the entrepreneurial personality. But you didn't really want to start a business, did you?

Total score = 18 to 22

You don't have the ingredients for entrepreneurship, but that shouldn't surprise you.

Total score = 23 to 24

Your entrepreneurialism may be adequate to entice employers.

Total score = 25 to 29

You have entrepreneurial talent sought by employers.

Total score = 30

You have plenty of entrepreneurial talent. Go for it.

6. Stress Tolerance

Add your scores for questions 2, 9, 16, 45, 83.   **TOTAL** _____

Subtract your scores for questions 23, 30, 37, 52, 60, 67, 77.   **TOTAL** _____

Your total score is: **TOTAL** _____

Total score = 5 or lower

Your poor ability to handle stress will turn away employers. Stress-management training would be useful.

Total score = 6 to 10

Your meager ability to handle stress won't attract employers. Stress-management training would be useful.

Total score = 11 to 12

Your ability to handle stress may be adequate to get hired.

Total score = 13 to 17

Your good ability to handle stress will be recognized by employers.

Total score = 18

Your excellent ability to handle stress will be prized by employers.

7. Leadership

Add your scores for questions 13, 20, 27, 34, 41, 49, 56, 64, 81, 88.   **TOTAL** _____

Subtract your scores for questions 6, 71.   **TOTAL** _____

Your total score is: **TOTAL** _____

Total score = 35 or lower

You have minimal leadership ability. Sorry, that's a fact.

Total score = 36 to 37

You don't have enough leadership ability to attract employers.

Total score = 38 to 45

You have adequate leadership ability for some employers, especially in a tight hiring market.

Total score = 46 to 47

Your leadership ability is apparent and will be recognized by employers.

Total score = 48

Your high leadership ability will be prized. Use it well.

Glossary

The following terms are frequently used in the field of psychological testing today.

Alternate form reliability.   A major method of determining a test's reliability. Individuals are given alternate (that is, highly similar but not identical) forms of the same test and their scores are compared.

Aptitude test.   A measure of individual ability in a specific domain, such as mechanical dexterity. These became important during the 1930s, particularly for vocational counseling and classifying industrial and military personnel.

Attitude test.   A psychological test that measures a person's attitudes in a particular domain, such as race relations or religion.

Bell-shaped curve.   See **Normal distribution curve.**

Construct validity.   See **Validity.** The extent to which a psychological test measures a theoretical construct or trait. Examples of such constructs are intelligence, verbal fluency, leadership ability, or anxiety.

Content validity.   Generally viewed as the most important method of determining validity, involving a systematic examination of test content to determine whether it covers a representative sample of the behavioral domain being measured. Achievement tests typically use this procedure.

Criterion-related validity.   See **Validity.** A method of determining a test's validity by comparing its scores to a specified, usually "real-life" criterion. For example, scores on a test of mechanical aptitude might be compared to actual job performance ratings of mechanics.

Extraversion.   See **Introversion.** Refers to a person's tendency to gregariousness and nonsolitary activity.

Five-factor model.   The most widely accepted current model of personality, encompassing the dimensions of neuroticism, extraversion, openness, conscientiousness, and agreeableness.

Frequency distribution.   A statistical method of grouping scores into convenient "class" intervals and tallying each score in the appropriate interval.

Group intelligence testing.   Group testing of intelligence was devised during World War I by the U.S. Army, under the direction of psychologist Robert Yerkes, to process recruits as rapidly as possible.

Integrity test.   A psychological test that measures a person's honesty. These are widely used in today's workplace.

Intelligence testing.   The first scientific test of intelligence was developed in France by Alfred Binet and his associates in 1905. It was known as the Binet-Simon scale and administered to children individually.

Interest test.   A psychological test that measures a person's interests, such as in various vocations or college majors.

Introversion.   A personality trait conceptualized by the Swiss psychiatrist Carl Jung, referring to an individual's tendency toward solitude and solitary activity. See **Extraversion.**

Ipsative test.   A psychological test in which an individual's scores are compared only with himself/herself, rather than on a continuum of high/low in comparison to others.

Multiple aptitude battery.   See **Aptitude test.** These are measures that assess a person's standing for several different traits, such as artistic, musical, and mechanical proficiency.

Normal distribution curve.   A statistical descriptor in which individuals' scores cluster near the center of the range and there is a gradual tapering off of scores as the extremes are approached.

Norms.   The standardized scores on a given test, such as the percentage of individuals whose scores fall within a particular range.

Percentile score.   The percentage of individuals who score at a particular level, or within a particular range, on a test.

Performance test.   A form of personality measurement in which the individual has a task to perform whose purpose is generally disguised. The earliest versions of such tests were devised in the late 1920s and early 1930s to assess children's honesty.

Personality test.   A psychological measure of an individual's basic characteristics such as his/her attitudes, emotional adjustment, interests, interpersonal relations, and motivation. Personality tests were first widely used during World War I.

Power test.   A psychological test that has a time limit long enough for everyone to attempt all items. The difficulty of the items is steeply graded; contrasted with a **Speed test.**

Predictive validity. See **Validity.** The extent to which a test predicts a person's subsequent success or failure in a given context based on his or her score.

Projective tests. Favored especially by clinical psychologists to measure emotional adjustment, these measures present the individual with a relatively unstructured task that permits wide latitude in its solution. This might involve describing ink blots, making a drawing, or telling stories about presented pictures.

Psychological tests. These are essentially objective and standardized measures of a sample of behavior.

Psychometrician. A person who is trained in the field of psychometrics. This typically requires a doctorate in psychology with a strong background in statistics.

Psychometrics. The scientific field of constructing and validating psychological tests.

Rating scale. Among the oldest form of personality testing, in which individuals are presented with questions and asked to respond on a point scale concerning degree of agreement or frequency of occurrence.

Raw score. A numerical score on a given test, meaningless without reference to the standardized norms for that test.

Reliability. Along with validity, the most important property of a psychological test. It refers to the consistency of scores obtained by the same individuals when reexamined with the same test on different occasions, or with different sets of equivalent items, or under other variable examining conditions.

Scorer reliability. A method of determining a test's reliability, in which two or more independent scorers rate an individual's responses. Such reliability is important in projective tests and tests of "creativity" where responses are more difficult to categorize.

Self-report inventory. Among the most widely used forms of personality testing, first developed by psychologist Robert Woodworth during World War I. The individual is asked to respond to a questionnaire designed to measure such aspects as attitudes, interests, emotional adjustment, motivation, or social relations.

Situational test. See **Performance test.**

Speed test. A psychological test in which individual differences depend solely on speed of performance. Such a test is constructed with items of uniformly low difficulty; contrasted with **Power test.**

Split-half reliability. A method of determining reliability, in which a test is split into two halves which are administered at the same time, and individuals' scores on the two halves are then compared.

Standard deviation.   A statistical measure of the variability of scores on a given test.

Standard score.   A raw score that is converted into a meaningful unit: specifically, the individual's distance from the mean in terms of the standard deviation on a given test.

Standardization.   Referring to psychological tests, this term implies uniformity of procedure in administering and scoring.

Standardized achievement tests.   Spearheaded by the work of psychologist Edward Thorndike in the early 1900s, these measure scholastic attainment in such areas as arithmetic, reading recognition and comprehension, spelling, and writing proficiency. After World War II such tests became an important admission criterion for colleges in the United States.

Test-retest reliability.   A major method of determining a test's reliability; the identical test is repeated on a second occasion and individuals' scores are compared.

Validity.   Generally regarded as the most important property of a psychological test. It refers to the issue of whether the test actually measures what it claims to measure. For example, does a questionnaire-format test of honesty actually measure a person's behavioral honesty in real life?

References

Arthur, Diane. *Workplace Testing: An Employer's Guide to Policies and Practices.* New York: American Management Association, 1994.

Csikszentmihalyi, Mihaly. *Finding Flow and the Psychology of Engagement with Everyday Life.* New York: Basic Books, 1998.

————. *Creativity: Flow and the Psychology of Discovery and Invention.* New York: HarperCollins, 1997.

Hoffman, Edward. The Right to be Human: *A Biography of Abraham Maslow,* second edition. New York: McGraw-Hill, 1999.

Hoffman, Edward (Editor). *Future Visions: The Unpublished Papers of Abraham Maslow.* Thousand Oaks, California: Sage, 1996.

Kroeger, Otto and Thuesen, Janet. *Type Talk at Work: How the 16 Personality Types Determine your Success on the Job.* New York: Dell, 1992.

Lambing, Peggy and Kuehl, Charles. *Entrepreneurship.* New York: Prentice-Hall, 1997.

Loehr, James. *Toughness Training for Life: A Revolutionary Program for Maximizing Health, Happiness, and Productivity.* New York: Plume, 1999.

Loehr, James and McCormack, Mark. *Stress for Success.* New York: Times Books, 1998.

Maggid, Renee and Codkind, Melissa. *Work and Personal Life: Managing the Issues.* Menlo Park, California: Crisp, 1995.

Matteson, Michael and Ivancevich, John. *Managing Job Stress and Health.* New York: The Free Press, 1992.

Minor, Marianne. *Preventing Workplace Violence: Positive Management Strategies.* Menlo Park, California: Crisp, 1995.

Murphy, Emmett. *Leadership: The Groundbreaking Program to Develop and Improve your Leadership Ability.* New York: Wiley, 1996.

Nanus, Burt. *Visionary Leadership.* San Francisco: Jossey-Bass, 1992.

Raber, Merrill and Dyck, George. *Managing Stress for Mental Fitness.* Menlo Park, California: Crisp, 1995.

Renesch, John. *Leadership in a New Era: Visionary Approaches to the Biggest Crisis of our Time.* San Francisco: Sterling and Stone, 1994.

Silver, A. David. *The Entrepreneurial Life: How to Go for It and Get It.* New York: Wiley, 1983.

Slimick, Tom. *Preventing Workplace Theft: They're Stealing from You.* Menlo Park, California: Crisp, 1995.

Tieger, Paul D. and Tieger, Barbara-Barrow. *Do What You Are: Discover the Perfect Career for You Through the Secrets of Personality Type,* second edition. Boston: Little, Brown, 1995.

Turkington, Carol A. *Stress Management for Busy People.* New York: McGraw-Hill, 1998.

Weisinger, Hendrie. *Anger at Work: Learning the Art of Anger Management on the Job.* New York: Morrow, 1995.

Index

Achievement motivation, 37
Adler, Alfred, 7, 8
Alcohol, 94
Allport, Gordon, 15
Anger, 61–67
    aspects of, 61–62
    hiring zones, 62
    sample test questions, 62–67, 105,
        112, 120, 129, 136–137, 145
    scoring method, 105, 112, 120, 129,
        136–137, 145
Antisocial behavior, 53–54
Anxiety, 93–95
Army Alpha and Beta, 13–14
Ascendence-Submission Test, 15
Attitude, positive, 95

Behaviorist approach, 7, 8
Bernreuter Personality Inventory, 15
Big Five model, 16–17
"Blacky Test," 4
Breakfast, importance of, 94
Bureau of Salesmanship Research, 13,
    14

Carnegie Institute of Technology, 13
Civil Rights Act (1964), 16
Coaching, 5
College Board, 5

Committee on Classification of
    Personnel, 14
Computers, 4, 6
Conflict, interview questions about, 23
Conscientiousness, 37–43
    aspects of, 37–38
    hiring zones, 38
    sample test questions, 38–43, 103,
        110–111, 118–119, 127, 135,
        143–144
    scoring method, 103, 110–111,
        118–119, 127, 135, 143–144
Cornell Science Index, 15
"Correct" responses, 27
Cultural issues, 11–12

Department of Justice, U.S., 61
Discrimination, in testing, 5–6
Drinking, 94
Drugs, recreational, 94

Educational Testing Service, 5
Enemies, interview questions about,
    24
Entrepreneurialism, 69–75
    aspects of, 69–70
    hiring zones, 70
    sample test questions, 70–75, 105,
        112–113, 121, 129, 137, 145–146

Entrepreneurialism (*Cont.*):
scoring method, 105, 112–113, 121, 129, 137, 145–146
Equal Employment Opportunity Commission (EEOC), 16
Erasing, 29
Extraversion, 45–51
aspects of, 45–46
hiring zones, 46–47
sample test questions, 47–51, 104, 111, 119, 128, 135–136, 144
scoring method, 104, 111, 119, 128, 135–136, 144

Five-point scales, 28
Freud, Sigmund, 4, 7, 8

Galton, Sir Francis, 13, 16–17
Guilford and Zimmerman Temperament Survey, 15
Guilford Martin Personality Inventories, 15

Halo effect, 14
Honesty, 53–59
aspects of, 53–54
hiring zones, 54
probing interview questions, 20, 21–22
sample test questions, 54–59, 104, 111–112, 119–120, 128, 136, 144–145
scoring method, 104, 111–112, 119–120, 136
Humanistic approach, 8

Integrity, 53–59
aspects of, 53–54
hiring zones, 54
probing interview questions, 20, 21–22

Integrity (*Cont.*):
sample test questions, 54–59, 104, 111–112, 119–120, 128, 136, 144–145
scoring method, 104, 111–112, 119–120, 128, 136, 144–145
Interviews, 19–25
general open-ended questions, 20–21, 22–25
probing for honesty/integrity in, 20, 21–22
Introversion, 45

Johnson, Lyndon, 16, 46
Jung, Carl, 4–5, 7, 8, 16, 45

Leadership, 85–91
aspects of, 85–86
hiring zones, 86
sample test questions, 86–91, 106, 113–114, 122, 130, 138, 146–147
scoring method, 106, 113–114, 122, 130, 138, 146–147
Lie Scale, 29, 31–34
sample test questions, 32–34, 103, 110, 118, 127, 134–135, 143
scoring method, 103, 110, 118, 127, 134–135, 143
Life events, 10
Life Insurance Sales Research Bureau, 15
Likert, Renee, 28

Major life events, 10
Management style, interview questions about, 24
Maslow, Abraham, 8, 16
Medication, 94
Minnesota Multiphasic Personality Inventory (MMPI), 15, 16
Motivation, interview questions about, 22

Motivational approach, 8
Myers-Briggs Personality Inventory, 4–5
Myers-Briggs Type Scale, 4–5, 16

Napoleon Bonaparte, 85
Nervousness, 93–95
Neutral category, 28, 29
Nixon, Richard, 46

Open-ended questions:
    general, 20–21, 22–25
    for honesty/integrity, 20, 21–22
Otis, John, 13

Panic, 94–95
Personality, 7–12
    changes in, 9–10
    formation of, 8–9
    interview questions about, 22
    measurement of, 10–12
Personality tests:
    computers and, 4, 6
    construction of, 11–12
    cultural issues in, 11–12
    discrimination in, 5–6
    history of, 13–17
    importance of, 4–5
    improvements in, 3–4
    nervousness before taking, 93–95
    privacy and, 6
    reliability of, 10–11
    sample questions (*see* Sample test
        questions)
    sample tests (*see* Sample
        personality tests)
    size of testing industry, 5
    test-taking procedures, 27–29
    validity of, 11, 12
Positive attitude, 95
Predictive validity, 12
Privacy, 6

Probing questions, for honesty/
    integrity, 20, 21–22
Psychodynamic approach, 7
Psychometrics, 9–10

Questions:
    Lie Scale (*see* Lie Scale)
    open-ended, 20–25
    probing, 20, 21–22
    skipping, 29
    (*See also* Sample personality tests;
        Sample test questions)

Rage (*see* Anger)
Recreational drugs, 94
Reeves, Russ, 45
Relaxation exercise, 95
Reliability, 10–11
"Right" responses, 27

Sample personality tests:
    instructions, 99
    practice tests, 100–103, 107–110,
        115–118, 123–127, 131–134,
        139–143
    scoring method, 103–106, 110–114,
        118–122, 127–130, 134–138,
        143–147
Sample test questions:
    anger and, 62–67, 105, 112, 120, 129,
        136–137, 145
    conscientiousness and, 38–43, 103,
        110–111, 118–119, 127, 135,
        143–144
    entrepreneurialism and, 70–75, 105,
        112–113, 121, 129, 137, 145–146
    extraversion and, 47–51, 104, 111,
        119, 128, 135–136, 144
    honesty/integrity and, 54–59, 104,
        111–112, 119–120, 128, 136,
        144–145
    leadership and, 86–91, 106, 113–114,
        122, 130, 138, 146–147

Sample test questions (*Cont.*):
   Lie Scale, 32–34, 103, 110, 118, 127,
      134–135, 143
   stress tolerance and, 78–83, 106,
      113, 121, 130, 137–138, 146
Sears, 15
Second-guessing, 29
Seven-point scales, 28
Skinner, B. F., 7, 8
Skipping questions, 29
Sleep, importance of, 93
Stress tolerance, 77–83
   aspects of, 77–78
   hiring zones, 78
   sample test questions, 78–83, 106,
      113, 121, 130, 137–138, 146
   scoring method, 106, 113, 121, 130,
      137–138, 146

Temperament, 8, 9
Test jitters, 93–95
Test-taking procedures, 27–29, 99
Thurstone, Robert, 15

Timed tests, 27
Trade tests, 14
Trick questions (*see* Lie Scale)

University of Michigan, 16

Validity, 11, 12
Violence (*see* Anger)

Watson, John, 7, 8
Weaknesses, interview questions
      about, 22
Woodworth Personal Data Sheet, 14,
      15
Woodworth Test of Emotional
      Stability, 14
Work setting, interview questions
      about, 23
Workplace Violence Research
      Institute, 61

Yerkes, Robert, 13–14

About the Author

Edward Hoffman, Ph.D., is the critically acclaimed author of *The Right to Be Human*, *The Drive for Self*, and *Future Visions: The Unpublished Papers of Abraham Maslow*. A licensed clinical psychologist based in New York City, he has over 20 years of professional experience with an emphasis on psychological evaluation, and lectures widely throughout the United States, Europe, and Asia.